CW00684896

art  of

ENTERPR SE

business toolkit

Art of Enterprise

Copyright © 2015 Phil Underwood. All rights reserved.
First paperback edition printed 2015 in the United Kingdom

A catalogue record for this book is available from the British Library.

ISBN **978-1-910546-00-0**

No part of this book shall be reproduced or transmitted in any form or by any means,
electronic or mechanical, including photocopying, recording, or by any information
retrieval system without written permission of the publisher.

Published by artof

Printed in Great Britain

Although every precaution has been taken in the preparation of this book, the publisher
and author assume no responsibility for errors or omissions. Neither is any liability
assumed for damages resulting from the use of this information contained herein.

v1.03

contents

A practical business toolkit
for entrepreneurs & enterprises

intro

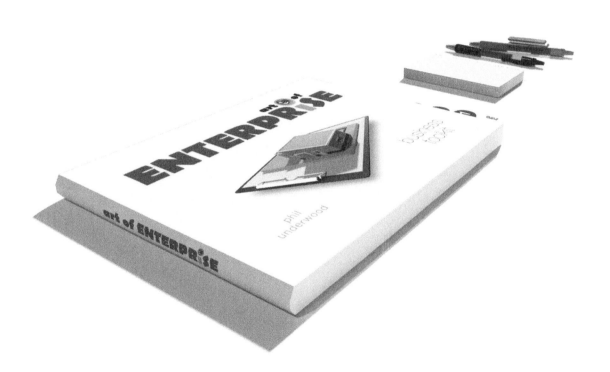

equip yourself

In a world that is changing fast, we need tools that help us discover, develop & achieve things for ourselves. Art of enterprise helps equip you with the tools you need for today & the future.

simple : just learn what you need, when you need it

There are two ways to use the book. To solve a problem just read a chapter, or work through the whole book to develop yourself. The aim is to help you to help yourself & inspire you to have a go.

solve
a problem

quickly identify your problem
& jump to that chapter for a
solution

develop
yourself

each chapter builds on the last
to develop your business &
leadership skills

case studies
real life applications

change
doing things differently

leader
developing leaders

people
understanding others

plan
how are we getting there

vision
where are we going

enterprise
where are we now

intro

how to use

The visual approach will bring learning alive & helps you to think in a creative & innovative way. Providing you with fast, accessible knowledge & with simple tools that help you develop ideas, businesses & yourself.

quick : all you need to know in a picture

The practical tools will provide you with fast solutions to common business challenges, all you need is a pen & a few stick its. Real examples from a variety of enterprises show the tools in action & show what is possible.

chapter

equipping &
developing yourself

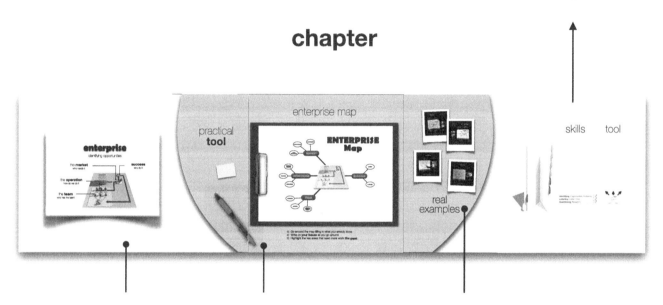

fast knowledge into a **practical tool** & demonstrated with **real examples**

real people in
real companies working on
real projects

business toolkit

The chapters are linked together to provide you with a development path & a comprehensive toolkit. Using each tool will help you develop new skills, enabling you to quickly improve your ability & performance.

useful : practical tools to solve real life problems

The final chapter looks at whole projects & shows the flexibility of the toolkit. The examples show how complex problems can be tackled, how ideas become reality & will hopefully inspire you to start your own journey.

toolkit

for fast & creative problem
solving

↓

SKILLS

Skill	
Inspiring (Role Model)	
Involving (Empower)	
Engaging (Empathy)	
Developing Others (Coaching)	
Learning (Seeks Feedback & Help)	
Self Awareness (Ability & Limits)	
Team Building (Collaboration)	
Influencing (Motivation)	
Interviewing (Individuals)	
Improving (Performance)	
Organising (Resources)	
Planning (Path & Priorities)	
Decision Making (Choices)	
Problem Solving (Create/Design)	
Analysing (Cause/Effect)	
Identifying (Opportunities/Problems)	
Listening (Collect Info)	
Questioning (Research)	

TOOLS

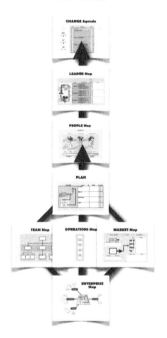

↑

business &
leadership skills

using the tools to
develop the skills you need

1
enterprise

enterprise

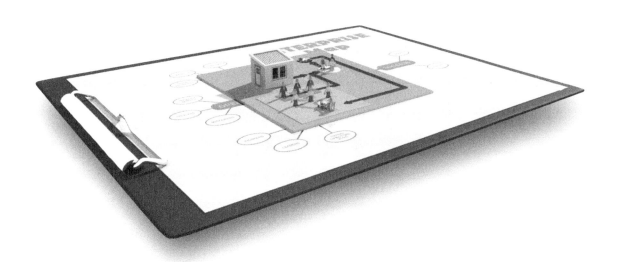

where are we now

enterprise

All enterprises are built in a similar way & contain the same core parts. By understanding the parts of our enterprise we will be able to see where we are. So let's take a moment & look at our enterprise objectively by :

☐ understanding **how enterprises work**
☐ organising **what we know**
☐ evaluating **the opportunity**/problems

After understanding the parts of our enterprise & how they work, we will be able to identify real problems, solutions & opportunities to grow. So let's explore our enterprise & see how we can make it better.

problem

1

where are we
now

capture &
evaluate an idea

identifying the
real problems

understand what is
happening

fast knowledge

An enterprise is a group of people working together (the **team**) to create a solution (the **operation**) that customers need (the **market**) & will buy (**success**).

Now let's turn these principles into a picture.

enterprise

where are we now

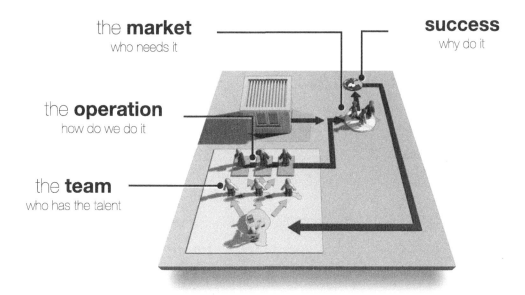

the **market**
who needs it

success
why do it

the **operation**
how do we do it

the **team**
who has the talent

the **team**
who has the talent

Enterprises are made up of groups of people working together. Specific talents are needed for each job, basically there are three sorts of job. **Workers** who are skilled at doing specific tasks. **Managers** who get results from people and **Directors** who are responsible for the enterprise & set it's direction.

worker

manager

director

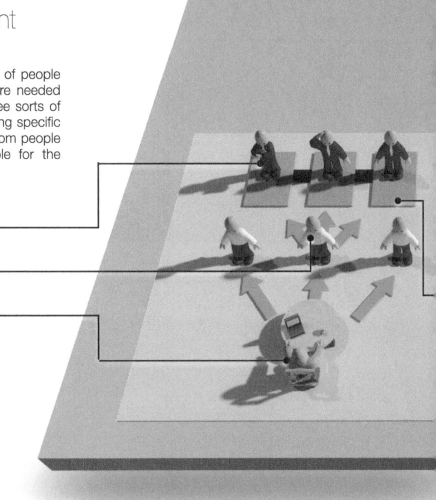

the **operation**
how we do it

The team carries out a series of actions to produce a **product** (a thing) or a **service** (helping or doing work for someone). They develop the best way to perform a series of tasks and capture this in a **process** to ensure a consistent output.

product/service

process

the **market**
who needs it

The products/services are bought and sold in a market. The solution solves specific problems for specific people, your target **customers**. If your solution is better or more affordable than the **competition** they might choose your offering.

customers ————

the competition ————

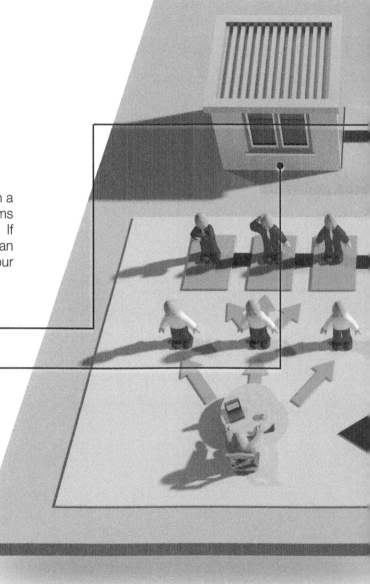

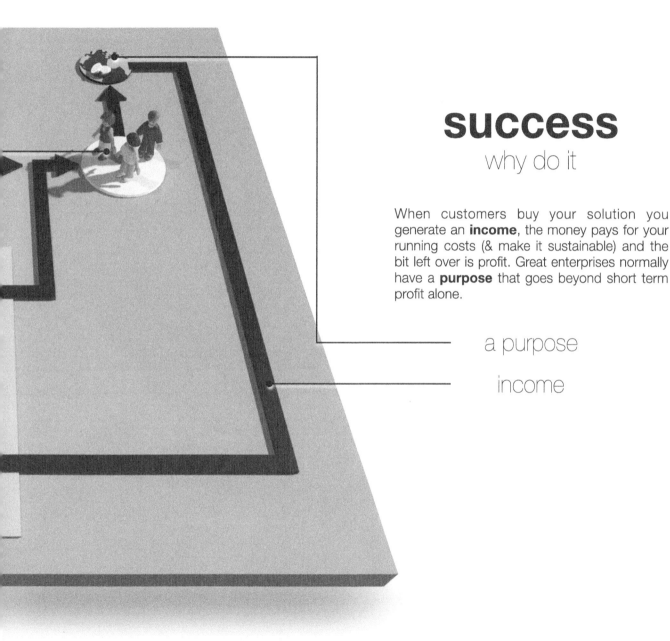

success
why do it

When customers buy your solution you generate an **income**, the money pays for your running costs (& make it sustainable) and the bit left over is profit. Great enterprises normally have a **purpose** that goes beyond short term profit alone.

a purpose

income

practical tool

Now we have an understanding of how an enterprise works and the four key parts.

This tool will help us visually organise all the information about our enterprise on 1 page. Allowing us to see our idea/enterprise clearly and work on it in a fast & flexible way.

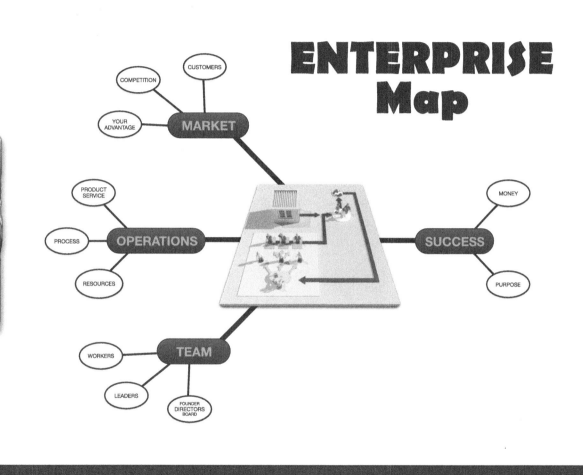

YOU CAN CREATE THIS TOOL BY JUST USING STICK ITS

ENTERPRISE Map

☐ Go around the map filling in what you **already know**.
☐ Write on **your issues** as you go around.
☐ Highlight the key areas that need more work (**the gaps**).

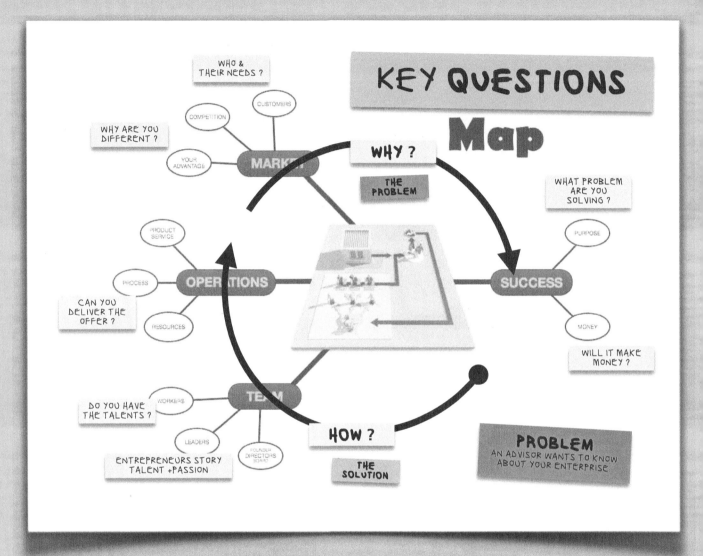

KEY QUESTIONS Map

WHO & THEIR NEEDS ?

CUSTOMERS

COMPETITION

WHY ARE YOU DIFFERENT ?

YOUR ADVANTAGE

MARKET

WHY ?

THE PROBLEM

WHAT PROBLEM ARE YOU SOLVING ?

PRODUCT SERVICE

PROCESS

OPERATIONS

CAN YOU DELIVER THE OFFER ?

RESOURCES

SUCCESS

PURPOSE

MONEY

WILL IT MAKE MONEY ?

WORKERS

DO YOU HAVE THE TALENTS ?

TEAM

LEADERS

FOUNDER DIRECTORS BOARD

ENTREPRENEURS STORY TALENT +PASSION

HOW ?

THE SOLUTION

PROBLEM
AN ADVISOR WANTS TO KNOW ABOUT YOUR ENTERPRISE.

use for...

Quickly capturing & evaluating a business, idea or project on 1 page.

tips

Good bosses, advisors etc will ask these questions, so be prepared.

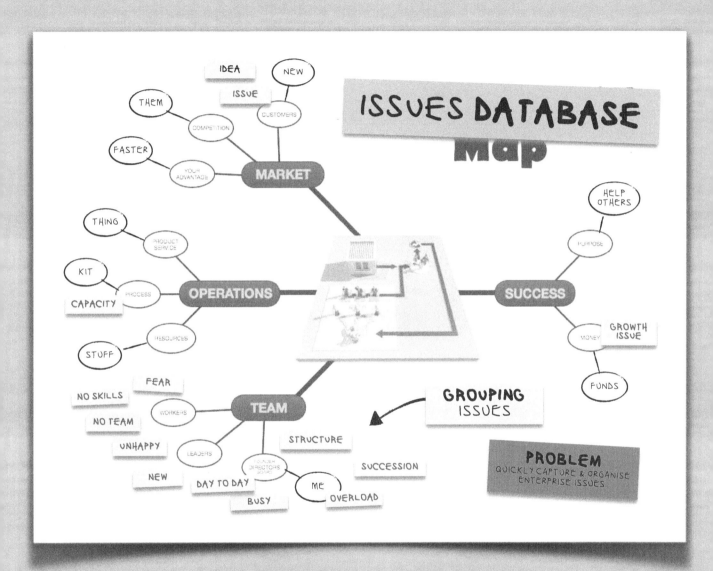

use for...
Collecting and organising (grouping) issues.

tips
Think about the real causes & be objective.

use for...
Identifying completed actions & where work needs to be done.

tips
Be realistic about your ability & understand the help you need.

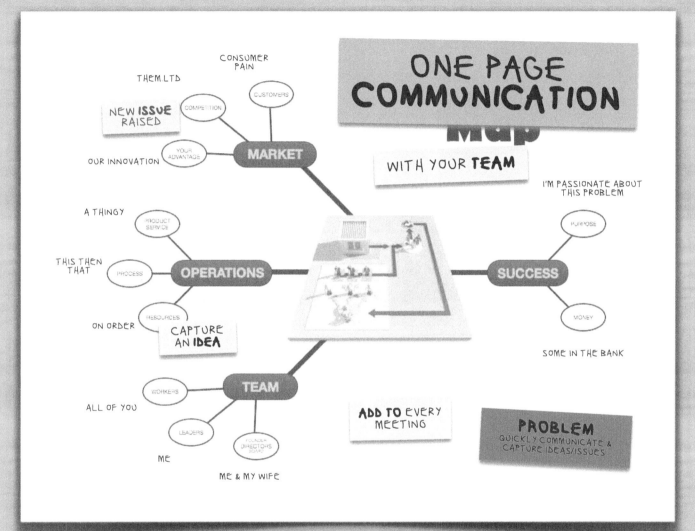

CONSUMER PAIN

THEM.LTD

NEW **ISSUE** RAISED

COMPETITION

CUSTOMERS

OUR INNOVATION

YOUR ADVANTAGE

MARKET

ONE PAGE
COMMUNICATION
Map

WITH YOUR **TEAM**

I'M PASSIONATE ABOUT THIS PROBLEM

A THINGY

PRODUCT SERVICE

PURPOSE

THIS THEN THAT

PROCESS

OPERATIONS

SUCCESS

MONEY

ON ORDER

RESOURCES

CAPTURE AN **IDEA**

SOME IN THE BANK

WORKERS

TEAM

ALL OF YOU

LEADERS

FOUNDER DIRECTORS BOARD

ME

ME & MY WIFE

ADD TO EVERY MEETING

PROBLEM
QUICKLY COMMUNICATE &
CAPTURE IDEAS/ISSUES

use for...

Communicating your idea/
enterprise to get resources or
recruit talent.

tips

Putting all your thinking on 1 page,
will help you stay focussed.

START UP

COMPANY TURNAROUND

SOCIAL ENTERPRISE

WORKFORCE RESTRUCTURING

Remember that this is a creative process and you continually add & change things. Reality often looks messy.

I'd encourage you to stick your work on walls, it a really quick way to get people involved & build on your thinking.

Now lets have a look at some real examples of the tool in action to solve a range of enterprise problems.

real
examples

Let's have a look at the tools & principles being used in a variety of different enterprises and on a range of problems :

- ☐ **start ups** - have lots of questions to think about, ideas to capture & communicate.

- ☐ **company turnaround** - have 1000's of issues to listen to & understand,

- ☐ **social enterprise** - they often have unique challenges/objectives & are difficult to review.

- ☐ **restructuring** - communicate to 100's of employees about new jobs.

KEY QUESTIONS
MENTORING A START UP

PROBLEM
To helping client see their idea/
enterprise objectively, understand what
they have achieved & what is left to do.

KEY POINTS
Areas that need more detail
(yellow highlighter)

**CAPTURING
THE BUSINESS IDEA**
Fast note taking & questioning to gain clarity.
Thoughts & solutions (black pen)

Record of the
meeting.

THE ENTREPRENEUR
Personal talents & roles
resources available (friends)
& help required (gaps)

PROBLEMS
Issues that need to be
worked on
(red pen)

SOLUTION
Tool used to summarise the
session & agree actions.

Young Entrepreneur with a **Business Idea** (2011)

PROBLEM
Find a fast way to capture & organise a large number of business & employee. Issues discovered during a company takeover.

ISSUES DATABASE
UNDERSTANDING A BUSINESS

CREATED
Enterprise map showing the challenges to be faced & the health of the enterprise

LIVING DATABASE
Map on the wall of the directors office with new issues & ideas added daily

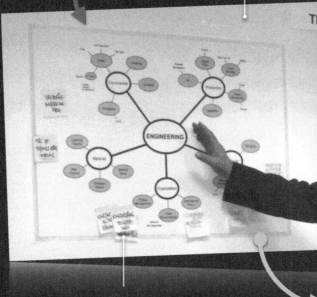

LISTENING
Identifying the hidden problems & their causes

SOLUTION
Created a wall that is key part of a series of workshops, involving up to 30 managers in validating the issues & develop a new (more relevant) business plan.

Listening & **Real-time Due Diligence** (2010)

PROBLEM

Help client to capture & communicate a
unique business model to all employees
(70% disabled) & stakeholders.

COMMERCIAL

Market realities & sustainability
challenges (move to break even)
providing more for less

**UNIQUE
BUSINESS MODEL**

Social purpose, community service &
commercial activities involving multiple
objectives issues & problems

Manager of x4 council
owned SMEs
(Supported Businesses)

CARE

Unique employee requirements &
employee development.
(adult care : public service)

SOLUTION

Communicate the business
model & business plan to
stakeholders.

Social Enterprise Business Model (2014)

COMMUNICATION
SHARED OBJECTIVES

PROBLEM
Developing a joint vision & buy-in for major
re-organisational by involving all employees
(1000 people) in the designing the future.

COMMUNICATE & CAPTURE
Main employee & union objectives including
new jobs, hour, pay & job losses

SOLUTION
Used in communication
workshops where 900
employees added their issues.

DEFINE & COMMUNICATE
Employer & business objectives including
commercial needs & work team culture

Workforce Restructuring Deal (1997)

31
enterprise

review

Now we have a simple picture of our enterprise, we are able to quickly diagnose issues, evaluate opportunities & review our enterprise in real time. Now you can :

start **identifying opportunities**

Keep using the tool as it will help you develop your questioning and listening skills. This research information will help you identify the new opportunities & the real problems.

enterprise

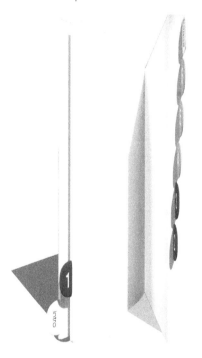

SKILLS		TOOL

Inspiring (Role Model)	
Involving (Empower)	
Engaging (Empathy)	
Developing Others (Coaching)	
Learning (Seeks Feedback & Help)	
Self Awareness (Ability & Limits)	
Team Building (Collaboration)	
Influencing (Motivation)	
Interviewing (Individuals)	
Improving (Performance)	
Organising (Resources)	
Planning (Path & Priorities)	
Decision Making (Choices)	
Problem Solving (Create/Design)	
Analysing (Cause/Effect)	
Identifying (Opportunities/Problems)	✓
Listening (Collect Info)	✓
Questioning (Research)	✓

practice using the
tool to develop
these skills

quickly capture &
diagnose issues

2

vision

vision

where are we going

vision

All enterprises need to have a clear vision of where they are going, a way of explaining what success looks like. To do this for our enterprise we need to look closer at the parts of our enterprise. So let's take a moment & start by :

- ☐ analysing & improving **the parts**
- ☐ **putting together** the parts to create designs
- ☐ assessing **the best design**

After looking closer at the parts & understanding how they work, we will be able to bring everything together to design a clear vision. So let's explore the parts & see how we can create a vision for our enterprise.

problem

2

where are we
going

| no direction | how to design the future enterprise | continuously improving |

fast knowledge

Understanding what customers need (**market** part), how it can be delivered (**operations** part), who will do it (**team** part) & the best way for the parts to work together (enterprise **design**)

Now let's zoom into the picture & explore these principles.

vision

where are we going

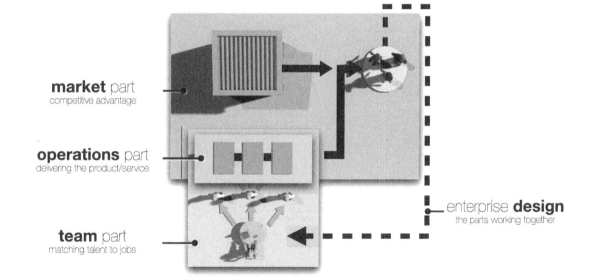

market part
competitive advantage

operations part
delivering the product/service

team part
matching talent to jobs

enterprise **design**
the parts working together

market part
competitive advantage

Identify who the people or enterprises are that buy your offer, split them into segments and define their specific **customer need**. Analyse the **competition** and why you are better than them. Then decide on your **route to market**, the best method to attract & distribute to customers.

customer need

competition analysis

route to market

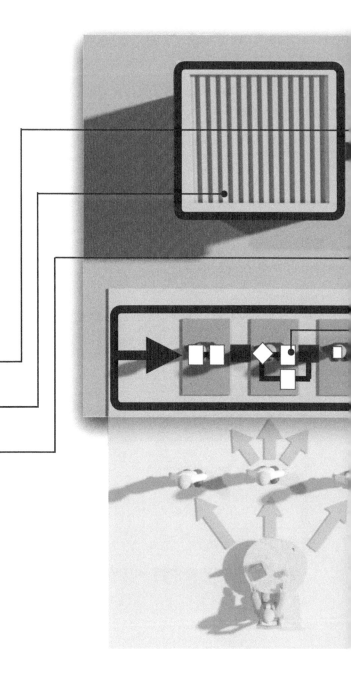

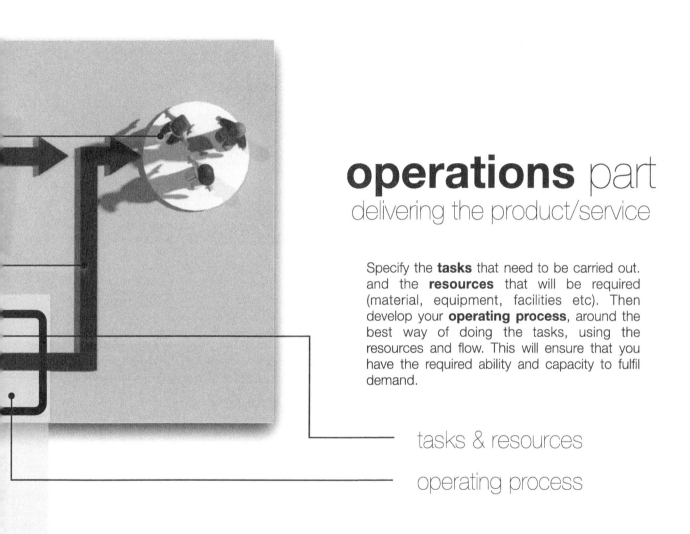

operations part
delivering the product/service

Specify the **tasks** that need to be carried out. and the **resources** that will be required (material, equipment, facilities etc). Then develop your **operating process**, around the best way of doing the tasks, using the resources and flow. This will ensure that you have the required ability and capacity to fulfil demand.

tasks & resources

operating process

team part
matching talent to jobs

Each person or group in the enterprise has responsibilities for tasks, which become **jobs** that their talents are matched to. The jobs are then linked together to create an **organisation structure**, with each link being a **relationship**. Each tier of the structure focusses on a different timeframe, workers minute/day, managers day/month and directors month/decade.

jobs

organisation structure

relationship

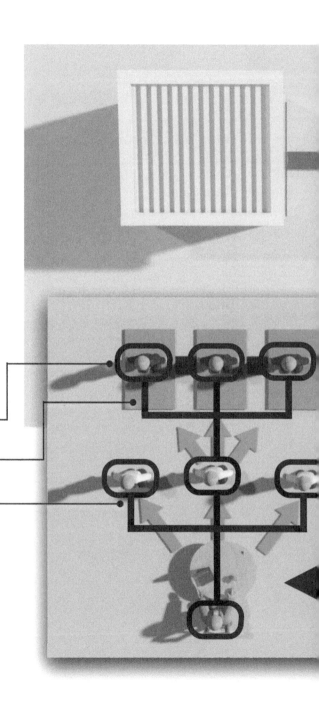

enterprise **design**
the parts working together

To be effective the three parts (market, operations & team) need to fit together. The **best design** (or fit) will enable the best team, to deliver the best solution, satisfy the customer & enable success. The design will have to be modified as the enterprises environment or size changes.

the best design

practical tool

Now we have an understanding of how the three parts interact and impact with each other. This is key to helping us design (or redesign) an enterprise.

The three tools that follow will help you look at each part in detail and visually organise lots of information, in a fast & flexible way & see reality clearer.

MARKET Map

YOU CAN CREATE THIS TOOL BY JUST USING STICK ITS

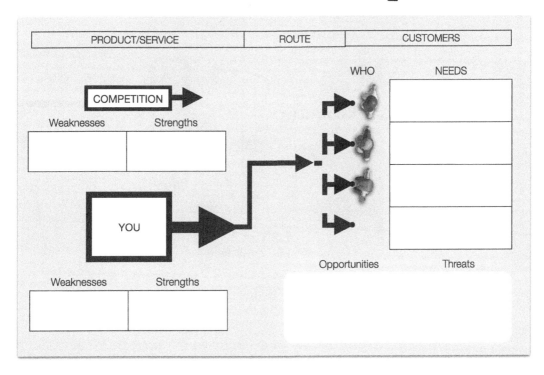

PRODUCT/SERVICE	ROUTE	CUSTOMERS

COMPETITION

Weaknesses | Strengths

YOU

Weaknesses | Strengths

WHO | NEEDS

Opportunities | Threats

☐ Identify **your** & the **competitions** strengths & weaknesses.
☐ Identify the types of **customer** & their **needs**.
☐ Write down any external **opportunities & threats**.

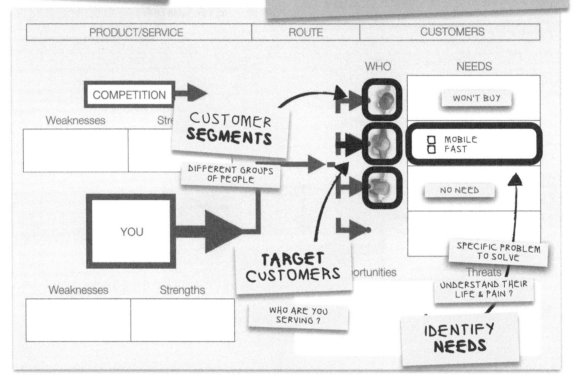

ARK

CUSTOMER RESEARCH

PRODUCT/SERVICE	ROUTE	CUSTOMERS

WHO   NEEDS

COMPETITION

CUSTOMER SEGMENTS

Weaknesses | Str

DIFFERENT GROUPS OF PEOPLE

WON'T BUY

☐ MOBILE
☐ FAST

NO NEED

YOU

TARGET CUSTOMERS

SPECIFIC PROBLEM TO SOLVE

...ortunities   Threats

UNDERSTAND THEIR LIFE & PAIN ?

Weaknesses | Strengths

WHO ARE YOU SERVING ?

IDENTIFY NEEDS

use for
Developing a living marketing plan & capturing customer/market knowledge.

tips
Talk to potential customers & listen to their feedback.

PROBLEM
IDENTIFYING THE COMPETITION &
HOW YOU COMPARE

MARK... COMPETITIVE ANALYSIS

PRODUCT/SERVICE	ROUTE	CUSTOMERS

WHO   NEEDS

(WHO ?)

Weaknesses   Strengths

NOT SO GOOD AT ?   WHAT THEY'RE BEST AT

OUR OFFER
PRODUCT & SERVICES

COMPETITIVE ADVANTAGE

WHAT MAKES US UNIQUE

Threats

Weaknesses   Strengths

NEED TO IMPROVE ON   WHY WE ARE DIFFERENT

WHAT WE ARE GREAT AT   KEY FEATURES

use for
Identifying your competitive advantage & what is unique about your business/offer.

tips
Your frustration with what is currently available can help shape your offer.

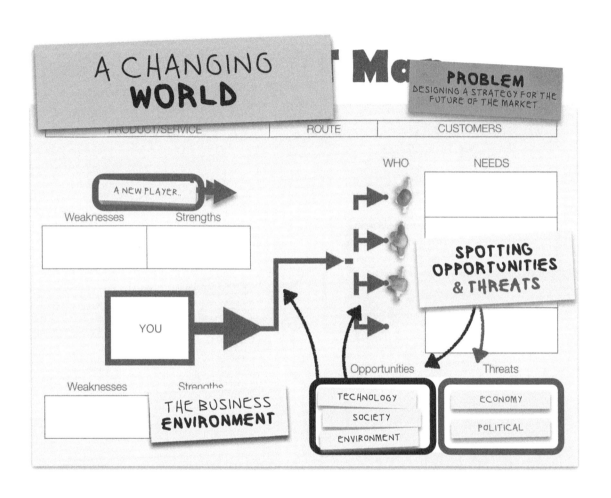

A CHANGING WORLD

...t Ma...

PROBLEM
DESIGNING A STRATEGY FOR THE FUTURE OF THE MARKET.

PRODUCT/SERVICE	ROUTE	CUSTOMERS

A NEW PLAYER..

Weaknesses | Strengths

WHO | NEEDS

YOU

SPOTTING OPPORTUNITIES & THREATS

Weaknesses | Strengths

THE BUSINESS ENVIRONMENT

Opportunities | Threats

TECHNOLOGY	ECONOMY
SOCIETY	POLITICAL
ENVIRONMENT	

use for

Capturing trends & analysing factors that can influence the marketplace.

tips

If you are innovating you can become a threat to others in the market.

ROUTE TO MARKET

Ma

PROBLEM
DESIGNING A STRATEGY TO TAKE
A ENTERPRISE TO MARKET.

PRODUCT/SERVICE		ROUTE	CUSTOMERS

WHICH CHANNELS

CO

Weaknesses | Strengths

PERSONAL
WEB
STORE

BRAND LOGO

COMMUNICATION
DISTRIBUTION
SALES

PUBLIC IMAGE
CUSTOMER
PERCEPTION

Weaknesses | Strengths

IDENTITY

Opportunities

REACHING CUSTOMERS

WHO | NEEDS

NO AWARENESS

USE
PURCHASE
AWARENESS

Threats

use for
Identifying the best way to reach
customers & your identity (brand).

tips
If you are the customer, how would
you discover & react to the offer.

PUBLIC SERVICE

START UP

INTERNAL CUSTOMER

SOCIAL FIRMS NETWORK

Remember all we are trying to do is learn as much as we can about our customers and gain some insight. We can then see if there's a product/market fit.

real
examples

Now lets have a look at some examples of the tool being used to solve a range of marketing problems. :

- ❑ **public service** - their customers are often hard to identify.

- ❑ **small business** - understanding it's strengths & competitive advantage

- ❑ **large enterprise** - identifying it's internal customers & become focussed & efficient

- ❑ **social enterprises** - discussing marketing options & their service needs.

PROBLEM
Understanding & profiling the current & future service users using market knowledge already within the organisation.

CUSTOMER RESEARCH
ANALYSIS

IN-DEPTH
Analysis on users & their needs

CUSTOMER PROFILING
Segmenting users

FUTURE
New users

library **market place**

library **community profile**

COMPETITION
Identify competition & market position

STRATEGY
Future directions to take the service

USERS
Who uses the service most

IDENTIFY
Individual customer needs & priorities

SOLUTION
Used to understand needs & trends of the service users.

Public Service Market (2003)

54
vision

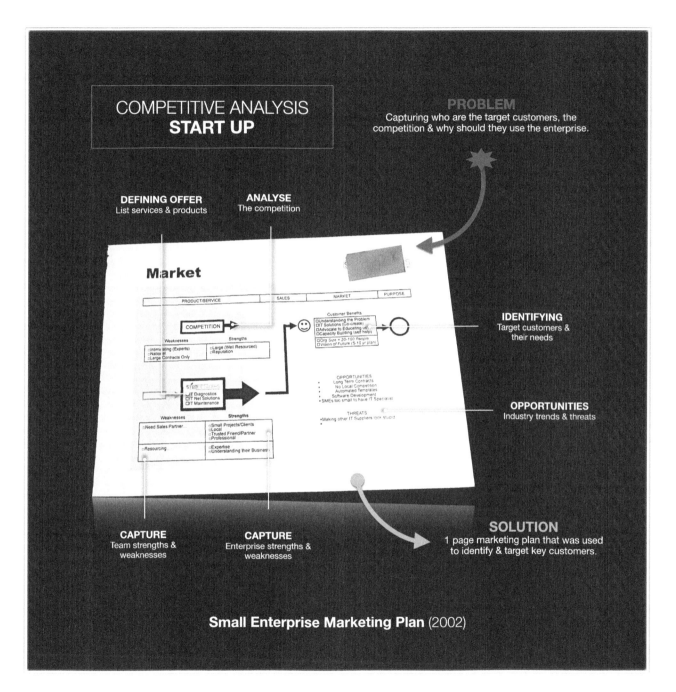

COMPETITIVE ANALYSIS
START UP

PROBLEM
Capturing who are the target customers, the competition & why should they use the enterprise.

DEFINING OFFER
List services & products

ANALYSE
The competition

IDENTIFYING
Target customers & their needs

OPPORTUNITIES
Industry trends & threats

CAPTURE
Team strengths & weaknesses

CAPTURE
Enterprise strengths & weaknesses

SOLUTION
1 page marketing plan that was used to identify & target key customers.

Small Enterprise Marketing Plan (2002)

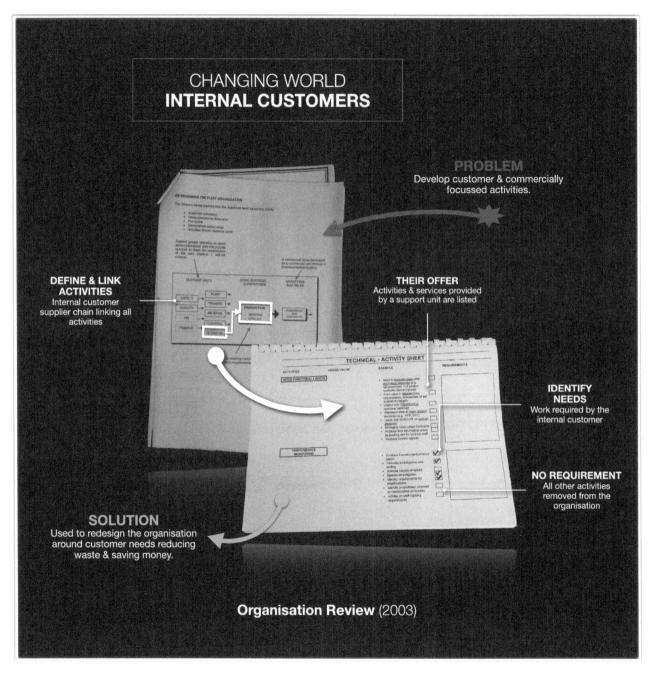

CHANGING WORLD
INTERNAL CUSTOMERS

PROBLEM
Develop customer & commercially focussed activities.

DEFINE & LINK ACTIVITIES
Internal customer supplier chain linking all activities

THEIR OFFER
Activities & services provided by a support unit are listed

IDENTIFY NEEDS
Work required by the internal customer

NO REQUIREMENT
All other activities removed from the organisation

SOLUTION
Used to redesign the organisation around customer needs reducing waste & saving money.

Organisation Review (2003)

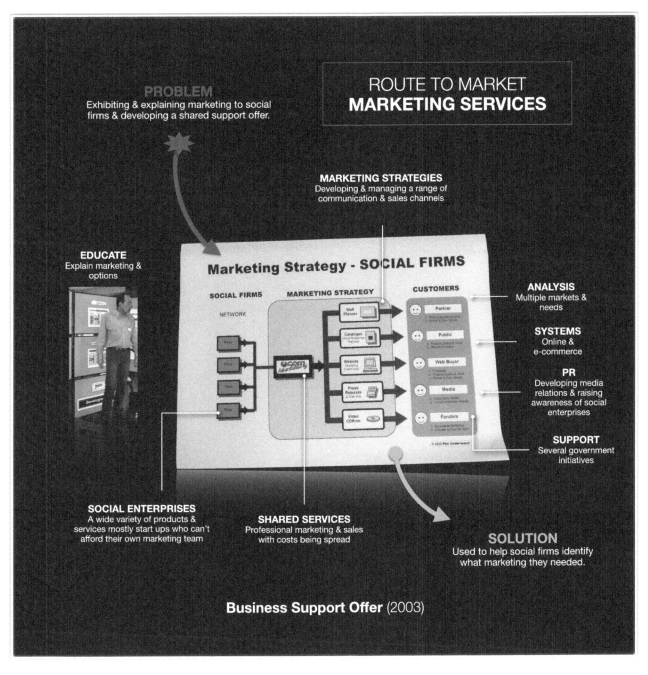

PROBLEM
Exhibiting & explaining marketing to social firms & developing a shared support offer.

MARKETING STRATEGIES
Developing & managing a range of communication & sales channels

EDUCATE
Explain marketing & options

ANALYSIS
Multiple markets & needs

SYSTEMS
Online & e-commerce

PR
Developing media relations & raising awareness of social enterprises

SUPPORT
Several government initiatives

SOCIAL ENTERPRISES
A wide variety of products & services mostly start ups who can't afford their own marketing team

SHARED SERVICES
Professional marketing & sales with costs being spread

SOLUTION
Used to help social firms identify what marketing they needed.

Business Support Offer (2003)

57
vision

practical tool

MARKET

↓

Once we've found a fit between the idea/ enterprise and the market we can start to design how we are going to deliver the product/service.

If it can't be delivered you need to go back to the market map & change the offer.

This is the tool that you will use the most, 60-70% of problems are caused by weak or non existent processes.

So master this one !!

YOU CAN CREATE THIS TOOL BY JUST USING STICK ITS

OPERATIONS Map

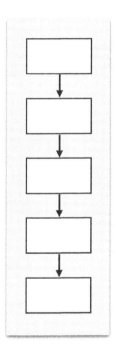

☐ Filling in each box with a task, ask **why** do this & **what** happens next.
☐ Now against each task add any **issues** or questions that need to be asked.
☐ Note any ideas or **best practice** & talk it through with others.

OPER MAPPING

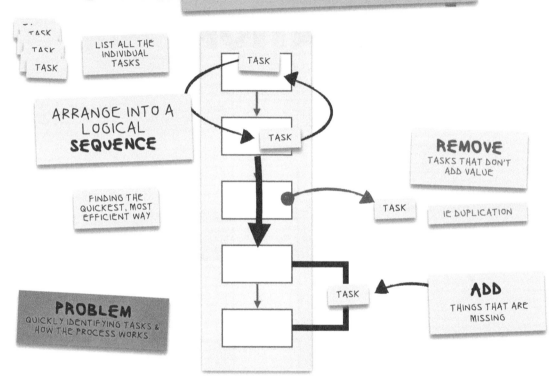

TASK TASK TASK

LIST ALL THE INDIVIDUAL TASKS

ARRANGE INTO A LOGICAL **SEQUENCE**

FINDING THE QUICKEST, MOST EFFICIENT WAY

PROBLEM
QUICKLY IDENTIFYING TASKS & HOW THE PROCESS WORKS

TASK

TASK

TASK

REMOVE
TASKS THAT DON'T ADD VALUE

IE DUPLICATION

TASK

ADD
THINGS THAT ARE MISSING

use for...
Quickly capturing a working process & core tasks.

tips
Most processes will be inside peoples heads, so try to get them down on paper.

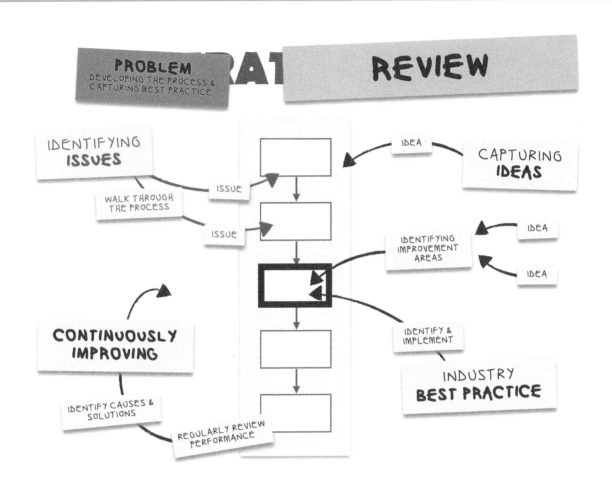

PROBLEM
DEVELOPING THE PROCESS &
CAPTURING BEST PRACTICE

REVIEW

IDENTIFYING **ISSUES**

WALK THROUGH
THE PROCESS

ISSUE

ISSUE

IDEA

CAPTURING
IDEAS

IDENTIFYING
IMPROVEMENT
AREAS

IDEA

IDEA

CONTINUOUSLY
IMPROVING

IDENTIFY CAUSES &
SOLUTIONS

REGULARLY REVIEW
PERFORMANCE

IDENTIFY &
IMPLEMENT

INDUSTRY
BEST PRACTICE

use for...
Improving a current process by
capturing issues & improvement
ideas.

tips
Listen to peoples feedback &
working knowledge to get best
practice/process.

61
vision

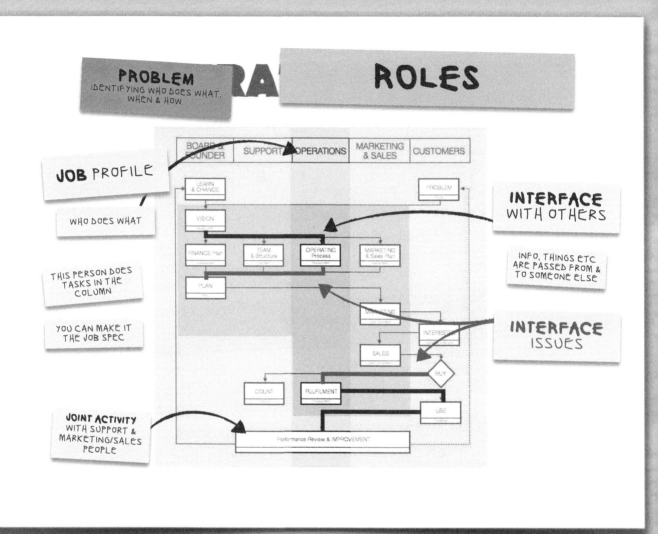

PROBLEM
IDENTIFYING WHO DOES WHAT, WHEN & HOW.

ROLES

JOB PROFILE

WHO DOES WHAT

THIS PERSON DOES TASKS IN THE COLUMN

YOU CAN MAKE IT THE JOB SPEC

INTERFACE WITH OTHERS

INFO, THINGS ETC ARE PASSED FROM & TO SOMEONE ELSE

INTERFACE ISSUES

JOINT ACTIVITY WITH SUPPORT & MARKETING/SALES PEOPLE

| BOARD & FOUNDER | SUPPORT | OPERATIONS | MARKETING & SALES | CUSTOMERS |

LEARN & CHANGE — VISION — FINANCE Plan — TEAM & Structure — OPERATING Process — MARKETING & Sales Plan — PLAN — MARKETING — INTEREST — SALES — BUY — COUNT — FULFILMENT — USE — Performance Review & IMPROVEMENT — PROBLEM

use for…
Adding job roles & assigning responsibilities to deliver the process.

tips
Somebody should own, be responsible for each process & it's improvement.

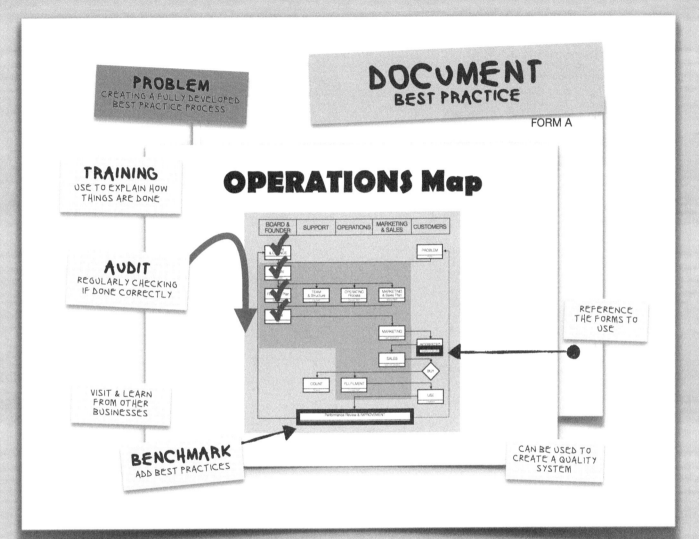

PROBLEM
CREATING A FULLY DEVELOPED
BEST PRACTICE PROCESS

DOCUMENT
BEST PRACTICE

FORM A

TRAINING
USE TO EXPLAIN HOW
THINGS ARE DONE

OPERATIONS Map

AUDIT
REGULARLY CHECKING
IF DONE CORRECTLY

BOARD & FOUNDER	SUPPORT	OPERATIONS	MARKETING & SALES	CUSTOMERS

REFERENCE
THE FORMS TO
USE

VISIT & LEARN
FROM OTHER
BUSINESSES

BENCHMARK
ADD BEST PRACTICES

CAN BE USED TO
CREATE A QUALITY
SYSTEM

use for...
Creating a procedure document to
ensure consistent approach &
outputs.

tips
Makes training new people &
sharing best practice easier.

TRANSPORT COMPANY

NEW IT SYSTEM

DOCUMENTING BEST PRACTICE

Remember what we are having to do here is build (or rebuild) something brick by brick, it means being very logical and walking through a process step by step.

If the process already exists we need to understand exactly how it works now & why things are done this way (it's normally for a good reason).

real
examples

Now lets have a look at some examples of the tool in action to solve a range of operational and process problems. :

- ❑ **transport company** - who's process is in the heads of several people.

- ❑ **company turnaround** - diagnosing & redesigning it's processes in real time.

- ❑ **new IT system** - how computers change the process & roles

- ❑ **large enterprise** - spreads best practice by documenting it's process into procedure.

MAPPING
A PROCESS

WHOLE PROCESS
Built up in 30 minutes

WHO DOES IT
Task responsibility

KEY TASKS
Stick-its for each key task

ISSUES
Added in red

IDENTIFY
Need to go deeper into this area & go talk to the workforce

IDEAS
For best practice

SOLUTION
Tasks & flow established with key improvement areas identified.

Directors Head (2005)

PROBLEM
Technical process to be reviewed by
30 managers & areas for improvement
identified.

REVIEWING
& IMPROVE A PROCESS

WEAK AREAS
Highlighted

STRUCTURE
One of four process maps that
described a whole department
of 400 people

CAPTURE
Key activities & areas that
need to be investigated
further

NEW IDEAS
Developed into solutions

IDENTIFY
Big issues that will
become major projects
they're not quick fixes

SOLUTION
Identified risks, redesigned
the process & created an
improvement plan.

Directors **Office Wall** (2010)

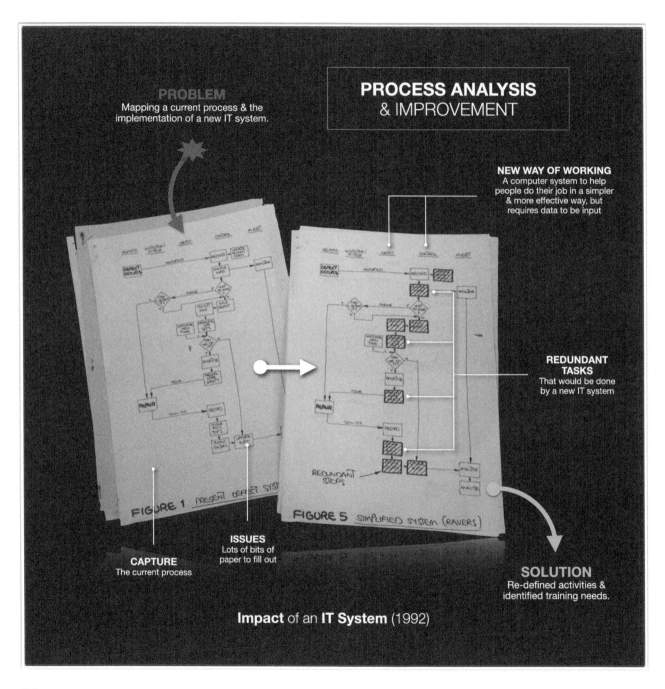

PROBLEM
Mapping a current process & the implementation of a new IT system.

PROCESS ANALYSIS
& IMPROVEMENT

NEW WAY OF WORKING
A computer system to help people do their job in a simpler & more effective way, but requires data to be input

REDUNDANT TASKS
That would be done by a new IT system

FIGURE 1 PRESENT DEFECT SYSTEM

FIGURE 5 SIMPLIFIED SYSTEM (RAVERS)

REDUNDANT STEPS

CAPTURE
The current process

ISSUES
Lots of bits of paper to fill out

SOLUTION
Re-defined activities & identified training needs.

Impact of an IT System (1992)

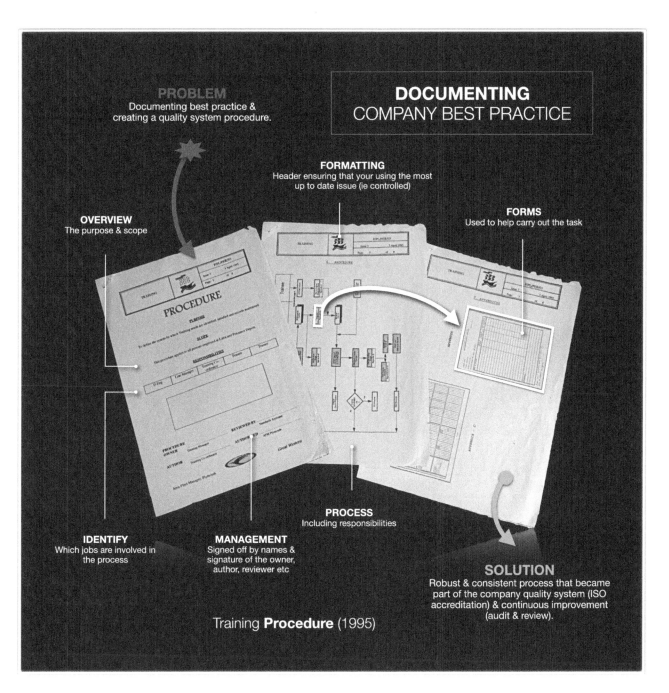

PROBLEM
Documenting best practice &
creating a quality system procedure.

DOCUMENTING
COMPANY BEST PRACTICE

FORMATTING
Header ensuring that your using the most
up to date issue (ie controlled)

FORMS
Used to help carry out the task

OVERVIEW
The purpose & scope

IDENTIFY
Which jobs are involved in
the process

MANAGEMENT
Signed off by names &
signature of the owner,
author, reviewer etc

PROCESS
Including responsibilities

SOLUTION
Robust & consistent process that became
part of the company quality system (ISO
accreditation) & continuous improvement
(audit & review).

Training **Procedure** (1995)

MARKET

↓

OPERATIONS

↓

Now we know what needs to be done we have to understand the talent required and the best way to organise it.

If the talent is not available we probably have to change our operation & possibly what the enterprise offers.

TEAM Map

YOU CAN CREATE THIS TOOL BY JUST USING STICK ITS

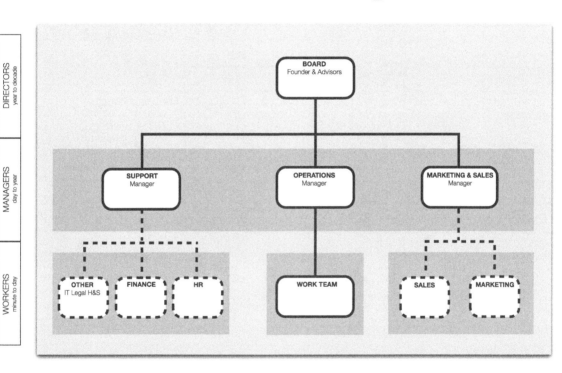

- ☐ Fill in the **names of the people** & their jobs.
- ☐ Draw in the **reporting lines**.
- ☐ Add on any job **issues** as comment boxes.

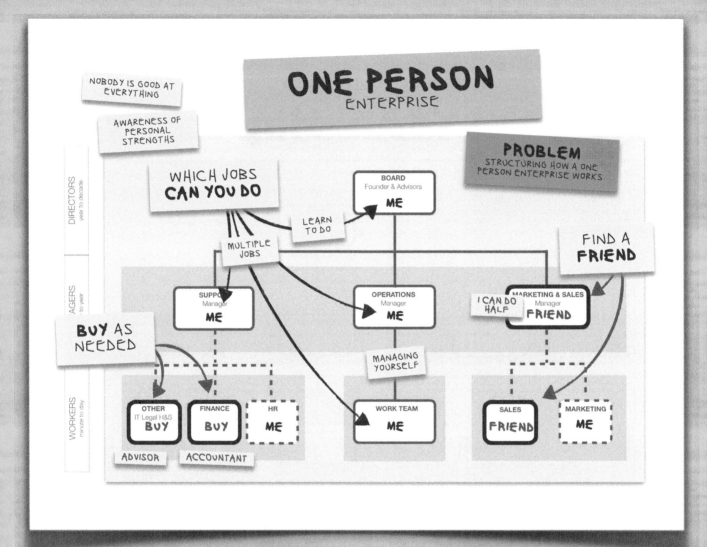

ONE PERSON
ENTERPRISE

NOBODY IS GOOD AT EVERYTHING

AWARENESS OF PERSONAL STRENGTHS

PROBLEM
STRUCTURING HOW A ONE PERSON ENTERPRISE WORKS

DIRECTORS
year to decade

WHICH JOBS **CAN YOU DO**

BOARD
Founder & Advisors
ME

LEARN TO DO

MULTIPLE JOBS

FIND A **FRIEND**

AGERS
to year

SUPPORT
Manager
ME

OPERATIONS
Manager
ME

I CAN DO HALF

MARKETING & SALES
Manager
FRIEND

BUY AS NEEDED

MANAGING YOURSELF

WORKERS
minute to day

OTHER
IT Legal H&S
BUY

FINANCE
BUY

HR
ME

WORK TEAM
ME

SALES
FRIEND

MARKETING
ME

ADVISOR

ACCOUNTANT

use for...
Identifying the individuals strengths & gaps in a one person enterprise.

tips
Build the enterprise around your strengths & find resources to cover the gaps.

TALENT
MANAGEMENT

WHERE ARE YOUR
BEST PEOPLE.

THE BEST **TEAM**
MATCHING RIGHT PERSON TO
RIGHT JOB

UNDERSTANDING
THE TALENTS
AVAILABLE...

DIRECTORS *year to decade*

MANAGERS *day to year*

WORKERS *minute to day*

BOARD
Fou...

D

PROBLEM
QUICKLY CAPTURING YOUR TEAM
TALENTS & ISSUES

BETTER
MATCH

PERSON PUT INTO
THE WRONG JOB

SUPPORT
VAL

OPERATIONS
JOE

MAR... ...LES
DAN

FC

FINANCE

TIM

PU

SUE

MARKETING

SUCCESSION
WHAT IF SOMEONE
LEAVES.. & THE IMPACT

GAPS
RECRUIT

use for...
Designing the best structure & team
around the talents in the enterprise.

tips
Think about an individuals potential
& how their talents could be used in
the future

73
vision

TEAM RELATIONSHIPS

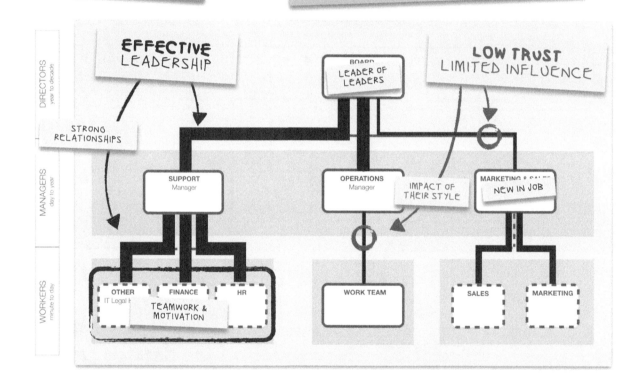

EFFECTIVE LEADERSHIP

LOW TRUST LIMITED INFLUENCE

STRONG RELATIONSHIPS

DIRECTORS
year to decade

BOARD
LEADER OF LEADERS

MANAGERS
day to year

SUPPORT
Manager

OPERATIONS
Manager

IMPACT OF THEIR STYLE

MARKETING & SALES
NEW IN JOB

WORKERS
minute to day

OTHER
IT Legal

FINANCE

HR

TEAMWORK & MOTIVATION

WORK TEAM

SALES

MARKETING

use for...
Assessing the relationships (trust) &
the health of the team.

tips
Take into account informal
relationships & who influences
whom.

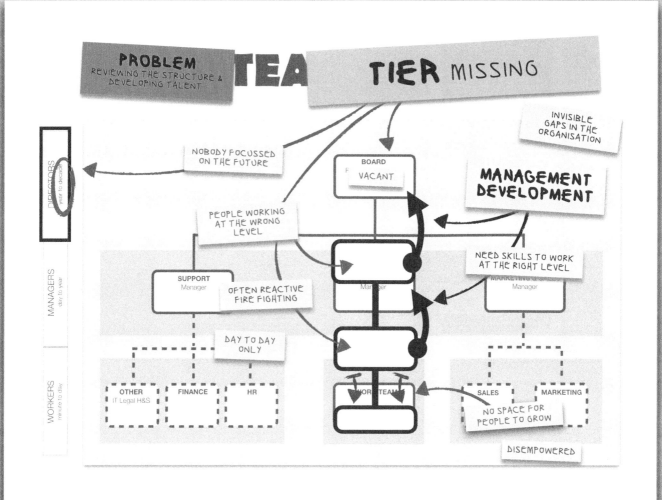

PROBLEM
REVIEWING THE STRUCTURE &
DEVELOPING TALENT

TEA... **TIER** MISSING

INVISIBLE
GAPS IN THE
ORGANISATION

NOBODY FOCUSSED
ON THE FUTURE

BOARD
VACANT

**MANAGEMENT
DEVELOPMENT**

PEOPLE WORKING
AT THE WRONG
LEVEL

NEED SKILLS TO WORK
AT THE RIGHT LEVEL

SUPPORT
Manager

OFTEN REACTIVE
FIRE FIGHTING

Manager

MARKETING & SALES
Manager

DAY TO DAY
ONLY

DIRECTORS
year to decade

MANAGERS
day to year

WORKERS
minute to day

OTHER
IT Legal H&S

FINANCE

HR

WORK TEAM

SALES

MARKETING

NO SPACE FOR
PEOPLE TO GROW

DISEMPOWERED

use for...
Identifying what managers are
doing & any development needed.

tips
A focus on day to day tasks, may
mean nobody is working on the
future

START UP

COMPANY TURNAROUND

WORKFORCE RESTRUCTURING

PRIVATISATION

Remember we are looking for the best way to organise the talent we have, not just for today but for tomorrow.

real
examples

Now lets have a look at some examples of the tool (principles) in action to solve a range of team & organisation structure problems. :

- **start up** - coping with growth by constantly developing its organisation.

- **large enterprise** - rebuilding it's organisation & redeploy talents.

- **workforce restructuring** - how 1000 jobs were changed & new work team created.

- **large enterprise** - where tiers were missing & had to be created.

PROBLEM
Constant redesign of the organisation as new clients & bigger projects mean the organisation has to grow & be designed around talents (strengths).

SMALL ENTERPRISE
& TALENT MANAGEMENT

NEW STRUCTURE
Drawn up, specific challenges, new roles required & structure shape

ORG MAP
Changing the managers roles

Re-Organising for Growth

Structure – Jan 08

Structure – April 08

Structure – Aug 08

ROLES REVIEWED
Identifying the existing strengths (roles performed well) & current weaknesses/gaps (where talents are required)

TALENTS DEPLOYED
Constantly developing the people & how they are used (roles/jobs)

CHALLENGES
Resources stretched & difficulty in finding new talent

SOLUTION
Designed structure & roles to explore the best way of using the existing talents.

Scaling Up the **Organisation** (2006)

PROBLEM
Review of the organisation & how talent could best be matched to jobs.

TALENT, JOBS
& STRUCTURE OPTIONS

CAPTURE
Formalised charts, adding job titles & consultation papers produced

ISSUES
Identified to be developed further with the team

MANAGEMENT
Reporting line issues & who is best to manage this person

SOLUTION
Organisation design & consultation proposal document.

DIRECTORS
Presenting first thoughts, explaining their diagnosis & thinking to 40 managers

COLLABORATION
Four groups worked to develop the thoughts/ideas & present back to other managers

Develop **Organisation Designs** (2010)

WORK TEAMS & NEW
RELATIONSHIPS

PROBLEM
An old organisation structure,
lots of jobs (trades) & little teamwork
with limited capability of delivering the
business needs (contracts).

NEW CULTURE
Major change to the way of
working, new relationships &
reporting lines

CREATE WORK TEAMS
New multi skilled jobs (4 grades) &
flexible teams responsible for
business activities

Old Organisation

The New Organisation

**CURRENT
STRUCTURE**
14 different jobs & trade
boundaries

With organisation chart
drawn upside to
emphasise that leaders
support the teams

LEADERSHIP GAP
Lots of supervisors with
technical knowledge but
few people skills

NEW TEAM LEADER ROLE
Major change in leadership style
with leaders developing &
empowering work teams

SOLUTION
Designed principles & new jobs
for a workforce restructuring
deal & implementation.

Re-Structuring Concepts (1997)

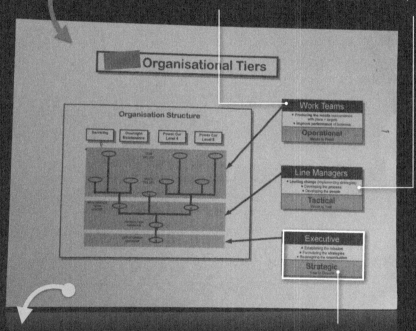

PROBLEM
No strategic or future focus
everyone was working on day to day.

DEFINE WORK TEAM
Identify the decision making (level of
empowerment) given to employees

DEVELOP MANAGERS
Middle managers to work on the week to
year timeframe & empower the work teams

SOLUTION
A bottom up design of the
organisation structure that would be
future focussed & flatter.

CREATE A STRATEGIC TEAM
Senior team to on the year to decade timeframe
& requiring commercial awareness/abilities

Organisation Design for a Privatised World (1995)

review

Now we have a simple set of tools that when used together can help us capture our vision & design the future. Or to quickly document and share best practice. Now you can :

create a **picture of the future**

Using these tools will help you develop your ability to analyse (understand cause & effect), solve problems (create & design) and make better decisions (select the best option).

vision

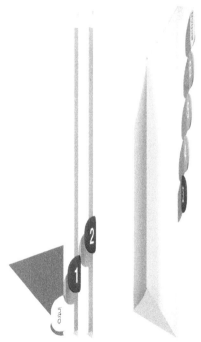

SKILLS

Inspiring (Role Model)	
Involving (Empower)	
Engaging (Empathy)	
Developing Others (Coaching)	
Learning (Seeks Feedback & Help)	
Self Awareness (Ability & Limits)	
Team Building (Collaboration)	
Influencing (Motivation)	
Interviewing (Individuals)	
Improving (Performance)	
Organising (Resources)	
Planning (Path & Priorities)	
Decision Making (Choices)	✓
Problem Solving (Create/Design)	✓
Analysing (Cause/Effect)	✓
Identifying (Opportunities/Problems)	
Listening (Collect Info)	
Questioning (Research)	

TOOLS

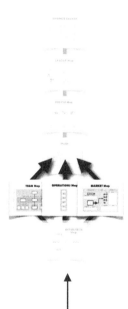

practice using the
tools to develop
these skills

using all three
tools to create a
vision

3
plan

plan

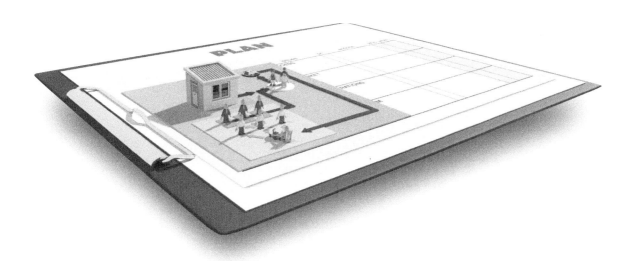

how are we getting there

plan

All enterprises need to have clear plans to function effectively. By understanding how to create, action & maintain our plans we will be able to optimise our resources & see how our enterprise is growing. So let's take a moment & look at :

- identifying a **logical path**
- organising your **resources**
- creating a **one page plan**

After understanding how to create plans, we need to use them to continually evolve & improve our enterprise. Our plans will help us stay organised, be strategic & track our progress. So let's explore how we can create effective plans for our enterprise.

problem

3

how are we
getting there

we can't do
everything

limited resources
available

who does what
& when

fast knowledge

Identify the steps that need to be taken (**issues & ideas**), decide on our route (**priorities & path**), then implement (**action**) & check if the plan worked (**review & improve**).

Now let's turn this knowledge into a picture.

plan

how are we getting there

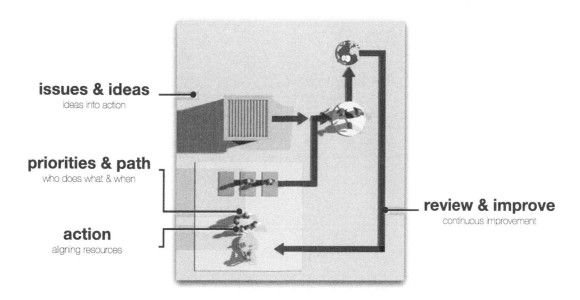

issues & ideas
ideas into action

priorities & path
who does what & when

action
aligning resources

review & improve
continuous improvement

issues & ideas
idea into action

To implement the vision you need to identify everything that is difficult to deal with or handle. **Group the issues** together, of which some will be guesses so we will need to try to identify the real causes not just the effects. Then we can **generate ideas**, develop solutions and actions for each issue.

group the issues

generate ideas

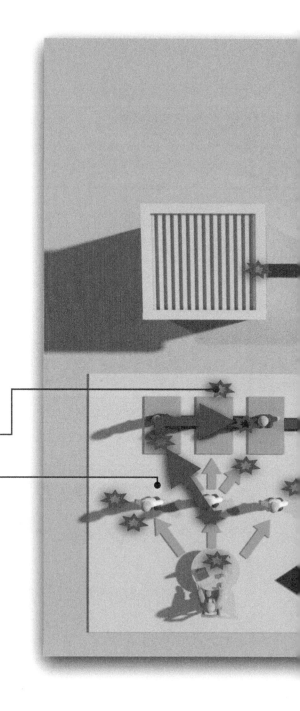

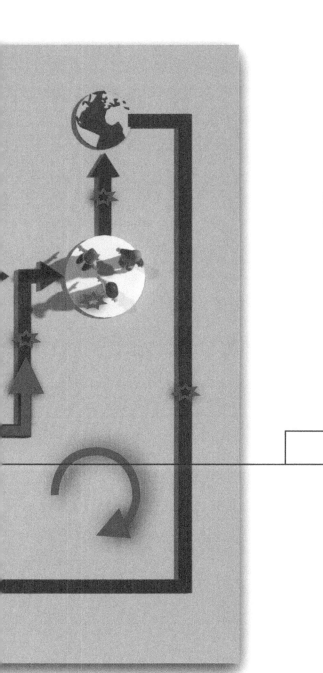

priorities & path
who does what & when

Find the logical sequence in which the actions should be carried out. Understand the skills required and **who** the best people are to accomplish the task. The size of the challenge will help identify how long it will take, **when** it should start/finish and the priorities.

who

when

action
aligning resources

To carry out what is required we need to let everyone involved know what is going to happen, so we create **a document** that brings together the what, when, who & how. We then use this to **communicate** what needs doing day to day & monitor how well it's going.

communicate

a document

review & improve
continuous improvement

To understand if things are going to plan we check that we are achieving results. We do this by defining good performance, setting targets and **monitoring performance**. By carrying out **regular reviews** we can spot trends, update the plan and continuously improve performance.

monitoring performance

regular reviews

practical
tool

We now have an understanding of planning and management. Remember management is how we coordinate the efforts of people to accomplish goals, using resources efficiently & effectively.

In practice plans are dynamic, they continually evolve, go wrong and get improved. But they help us stay organised, be strategic and track progress.

PLAN

YOU CAN CREATE THIS TOOL BY JUST USING STICK ITS

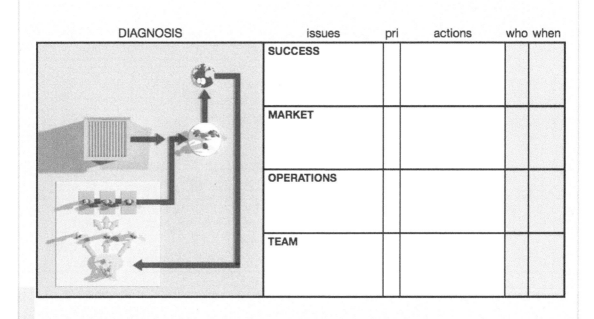

DIAGNOSIS	issues	pri	actions	who	when
	SUCCESS				
	MARKET				
	OPERATIONS				
	TEAM				

- ☐ Put **issues** into the relevant Team, Operations, Market & Success boxes.
- ☐ Look at each **issue** & opposite each develop **actions** to solve it.
- ☐ Against each action identify **who** should take action & **when**.

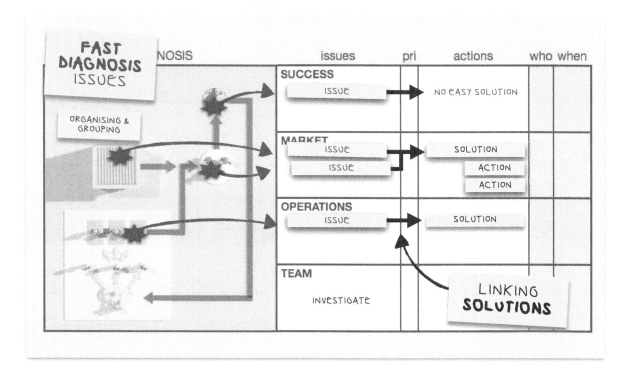

ISSUES + ACTIONS

FAST DIAGNOSIS ISSUES

...NOSIS

ORGANISING & GROUPING

	issues	pri	actions	who	when
SUCCESS	ISSUE		NO EASY SOLUTION		
MARKET	ISSUE		SOLUTION		
	ISSUE		ACTION		
			ACTION		
OPERATIONS	ISSUE		SOLUTION		
TEAM	INVESTIGATE				

LINKING **SOLUTIONS**

use for...

Quick one page plan identifying
issues & capturing actions to solve
them.

tips

Plans are living things, so
continually add issues & test your
diagnosis.

THE BEST PATH

PROBLEM
DESIGNING THE BEST WAY TO
IMPLEMENT PLAN

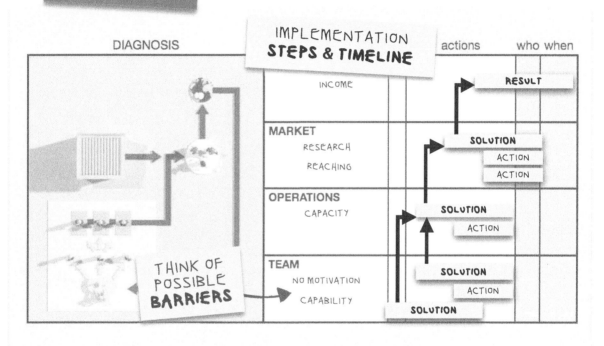

DIAGNOSIS

IMPLEMENTATION
STEPS & TIMELINE

actions   who when

INCOME

RESULT

MARKET
RESEARCH
REACHING

SOLUTION
ACTION
ACTION

OPERATIONS
CAPACITY

SOLUTION
ACTION

THINK OF
POSSIBLE
BARRIERS

TEAM
NO MOTIVATION
CAPABILITY

SOLUTION
ACTION

SOLUTION

use for...

Identifying the steps & barriers to
implementing a solution.

tips

The longest sequence of activities
in the plan will determine the
completion time.

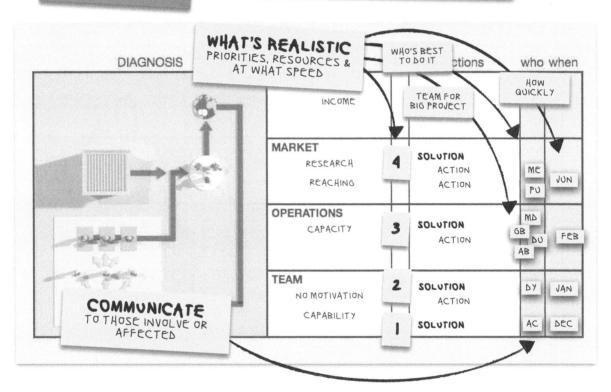

PLAN OF **ACTION**

PROBLEM
CAPTURING ACTIONS, GAPS, ISSUES & SOLUTIONS.

WHAT'S REALISTIC
PRIORITIES, RESOURCES & AT WHAT SPEED

WHO'S BEST TO DO IT

DIAGNOSIS ...ctions who when

HOW QUICKLY

INCOME

TEAM FOR BIG PROJECT

MARKET	4	**SOLUTION**	ME	JUN
RESEARCH		ACTION		
REACHING		ACTION	PU	
OPERATIONS	3	**SOLUTION**	MD	FEB
CAPACITY		ACTION	GB DU	
			AB	
TEAM	2	**SOLUTION**	DY	JAN
NO MOTIVATION		ACTION		
CAPABILITY	1	**SOLUTION**	AC	DEC

COMMUNICATE
TO THOSE INVOLVE OR AFFECTED

use for...
Defining individual responsibilities & priorities.

tips
Think about the capability of those involved & their motivation.

PLAN PROGRESS

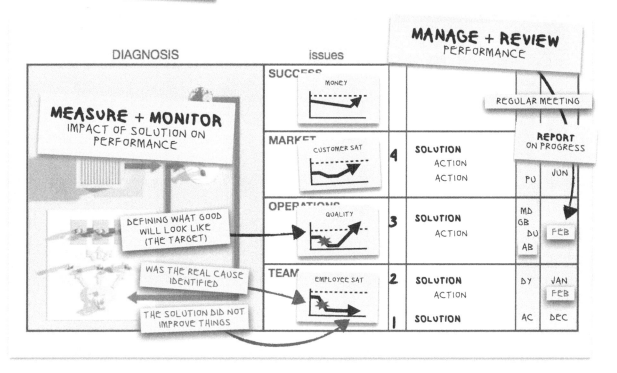

use for...

Reviewing that a plan is working, by identifying performance measures & targets.

tips

Create graphs to track performance & to help spot trends.

EMPLOYEE INVOLVEMENT

START UP

LARGE ENTERPRISE

PROJECT REPORT

Remember what we are doing is planning a route in advance. It's about being prepared and being able to respond to unforeseen problems or opportunities.

A couple of the examples show tools from chapter 2 being used to develop a plan.

real
examples

Now lets have a look at some examples of the tool (& principles) in action to solve a range of problems. :

☐ **improvement teams** - shop floor teams identifying problems & implementing solutions.

☐ **small IT business** - stayed focussed with a one page business plan.

☐ **large enterprise** - an event where 120 managers were involved in action planning.

☐ **complex project** - the plan becomes a progress report.

IMPROVEMENT TEAM
ISSUES & ACTIONS

PROBLEM
Involving employees in improving the business ten teams quickly identifying issues & implementing ideas.

OBJECTIVE
Problem statement & team remit

PARTICIPANTS
Team members (volunteers) from the shopfloor

SIZE OF THE PROBLEM
What the problem was costing

ISSUES DEFINED
Effects linked to causes and issues identified & grouped

ACTION PLANNED
Solutions proposed and prototypes designed, made & tested by the team

IMPLEMENTATION & COMMUNICATION
Equipment before & after photos

SOLUTION
Problems solved, ownership of an improvement plan & continuous improvement by all employees.

Shopfloor Quality Improvement Team (1990)

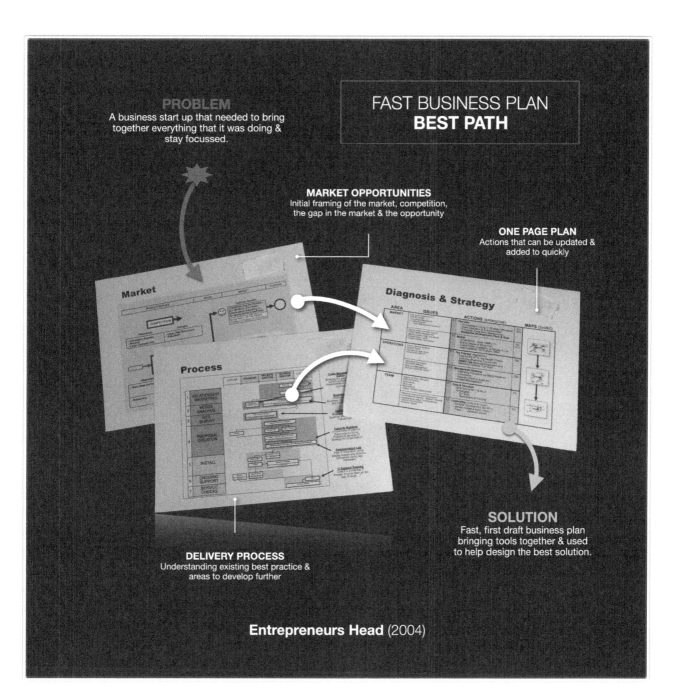

LEADERS **COMMUNICATING** A BUSINESS PLAN

PROBLEM
Fast communication of plans & the involvement of 120 managers in developing the business.

INITIAL PLANS
Specific business goals (two of the six) that is working/living document

FAST COMMUNICATION & CAPTURE
Used as posters at management conferences, with cross functional groups discussing the plans identifying more issues & generating ideas

ISSUES & ACTIONS
Challenges grouped to become projects with a logical sequence of actions

SOLUTION
Validating the challenges, capturing more issues, ideas, creating a better plan and implementation buy in of 120 managers.

Plans Developed by **120 Leaders** (2000)

PROBLEM
Reviewed performance process & created
an action plan with recommendations.

PROJECT REPORT &
PROGRESS TRACKING

DOCUMENT & TRACKING
All brought together as a report, next
steps recommended & actioned

**PERFORMANCE
MONITORING SOLUTIONS**
Developed for each issue to explain
what it might look like

**FAST
COMMUNICATION**
The plan & collecting
the thoughts of others

ISSUES
Identified by mapping
the process

PRIORITIES
Based on the best way of
developing the process

SOLUTION
Created a full report that was communicated,
implemented & improved performance.

Performance Improvement **Action Plan** (2010)

review

With this plan is a flexible document that helps us to establish priorities, communicate actions, align our resources & review our progress effectively. Now you can :

develop **a strategy**

Using this tool will help you develop your ability to plan (identify the best path & task priorities), organise (talent & resources) and continuously improve (performance & the plan).

plan

SKILLS

Inspiring (Role Model)
Involving (Empower)
Engaging (Empathy)

Developing Others (Coaching)
Learning (Seeks Feedback & Help)
Self Awareness (Ability & Limits)

Team Building (Collaboration)
Influencing (Motivation)
Interviewing (Individuals)

Improving (Performance)	✓
Organising (Resources)	✓
Planning (Path & Priorities)	✓

Decision Making (Choices)
Problem Solving (Create/Design)
Analysing (Cause/Effect)

Identifying (Opportunities/Problems)
Listening (Collect Info)
Questioning (Research)

TOOL

practice using the
tool to develop
these skills

one page plan

4

people

people

understanding others

people

All enterprises contain different jobs requiring different talents. This means we have to learn & understand how to get the best out of our people & make the most of their different abilities & viewpoints. So let's start :

- ❑ understanding **individual** uniqueness
- ❑ identifying how **engaged people** are
- ❑ deciding the required **culture** & **leadership**

After understanding how people work, we need to look at our people to identify how they work individually, as a team & how we can help them to achieve their potential. So let's explore our enterprise & see how we can make our people perform better.

problem

4

understanding others

engaging employees

unlocking employee potential

what does good leadership look like

fast knowledge

Find out what people are good at (**talent**), what they need (**motivation**), match them to a job (**teamwork**) & then empower them (**leadership styles**).

Now let's zoom in to our picture

people
understanding others

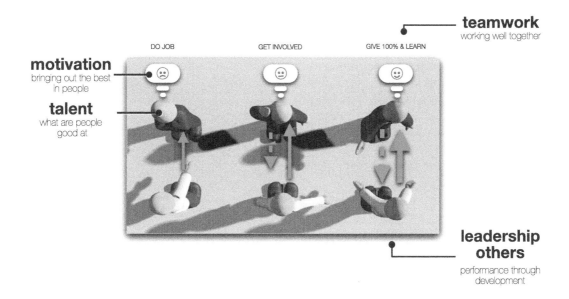

teamwork
working well together

motivation
bringing out the best
in people

talent
what are people
good at

DO JOB   GET INVOLVED   GIVE 100% & LEARN

**leadership
others**
performance through
development

talent
what are people good at

Every individual has natural abilities, **talents** & the **potential** to develop those or other abilities. Recruitment is **job matching** and involves identifying what you need for a job & finding the right person. Job matching never really stops, because as people develop (realise their potential) they will be able to do other jobs.

talent & potential

job matching

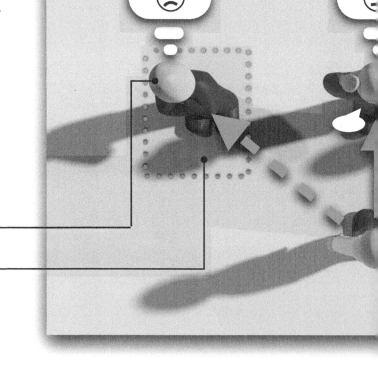

DO JOB

GET IN

GIVE 100% & LEARN

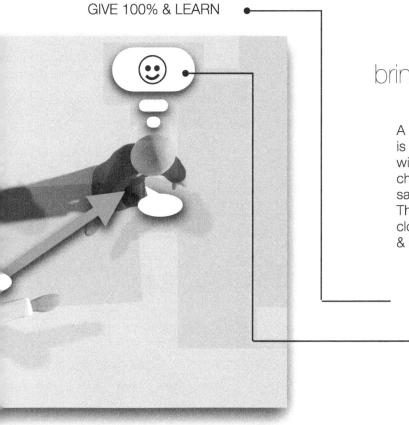

motivation
bringing out the best in people

A couple of factors will determine if a person
is motivated to do their best. Each individual
will decide their **level of engagement**,
choosing between just do the job (don't get
sacked), get involved or give 100% & learn.
The second factor is **job satisfaction**, how
close the job matches what they are good at
& love to do.

level of engagement

job satisfaction

teamwork
working well together

Teamwork is about getting the right people to co-operate in achieving a common goal. The **business need** (goal) can be simply compliance or at the other extreme be talent retention & innovation. This need will determine how things are done, how decisions are made, normal behaviours and **the culture** within the enterprise.

business need

the culture

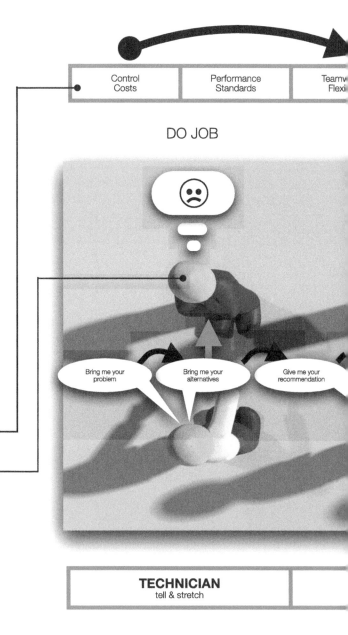

Control Costs	Performance Standards	Teamw Flexi

DO JOB

Bring me your problem

Bring me your alternatives

Give me your recommendation

TECHNICIAN
tell & stretch

Continuous Improvement	Retain & Utilise Talent	Innovation & Change

VOLVED   GIVE 100% & LEARN

AGER	LEADER
involve	delegate & coach

leading others

performance through development

Leading is about maximising the contribution of others. The involvement is the most effective approach, **empowering** people to take action, openly share their knowledge & experience. Different **leadership styles** will be useful for different development stages, situations & individuals. The bigger our range of styles the more effective we will be.

empowering

leadership styles

practical tool

Now we can take our understanding of people & load all of the information onto 1 page. Then we'll see how the tool can be used to solve four common problems.

YOU CAN CREATE
THIS TOOL BY JUST
USING STICK ITS

PEOPLE Map

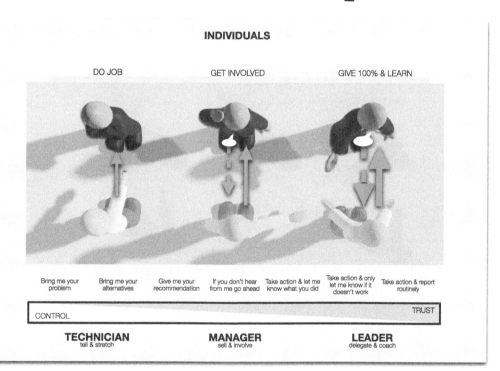

INDIVIDUALS

DO JOB	GET INVOLVED	GIVE 100% & LEARN

Bring me your problem	Bring me your alternatives	Give me your recommendation	If you don't hear from me go ahead	Take action & let me know what you did	Take action & only let me know if it doesn't work	Take action & report routinely

CONTROL ⟶ TRUST

TECHNICIAN tell & stretch	**MANAGER** sell & involve	**LEADER** delegate & coach

☐ Identify where **individuals** (your team) are on the motivation line.
☐ Add where you think **you are** on the leadership style bar.
☐ Get **your team** to identify on the bar your leadership style.

PEOPLE Map

PROBLEM
CAPTURING WHERE THE TEAM IS & THEIR MOTIVATIONS.

☹ J ☹ T ☺ RS   ...DIVIDUALS

DO JOB   GET INVOLVED   GIVE 100% & LEARN

☹ P

GOOD PEOPLE MAY WANT TO LEAVE

☹ N

DISCOVER THE REAL ISSUES

LISTEN

HOW WOULD YOU FEEL IF YOU WERE THEM

HOW ARE PEOPLE FEELING

Bring me yo... problem

...on & only ...now if it ...t work

Take action & report routinely

EMPLOYEE ENGAGEMENT

CONTROL   TRUST

TE...   ...LEADER
                               delegate & coach

use for...
Identifying the level of employee engagement & their motivation.

tips
Put yourself in the employees position & think about how you would feel.

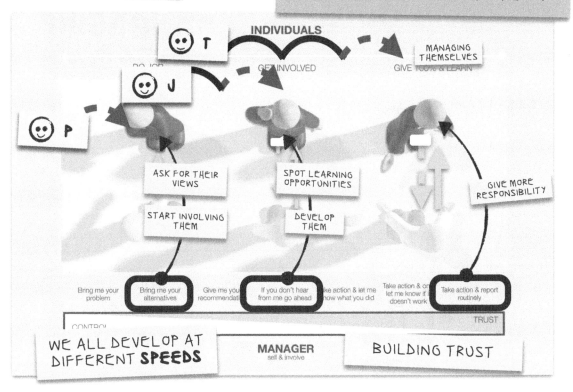

PROBLEM
IDENTIFYING TEAM LEADERSHIP, ISSUES & DEVELOPMENTS

DELEGATION
& TEAM DEVELOPMENT

INDIVIDUALS

DO JOB · GET INVOLVED · GIVE 100% & LEARN

MANAGING THEMSELVES

T

J

P

| ASK FOR THEIR VIEWS | SPOT LEARNING OPPORTUNITIES | GIVE MORE RESPONSIBILITY |
| START INVOLVING THEM | DEVELOP THEM | |

Bring me your problem · Bring me your alternatives · Give me your recommendation · If you don't hear from me go ahead · Take action & let me know what you did · Take action & on let me know if it doesn't work · Take action & report routinely

CONTROL — TRUST

WE ALL DEVELOP AT DIFFERENT **SPEEDS**

MANAGER
self & involve

BUILDING TRUST

use for…
Managing the development of teams & individuals.

tips
Delegation is not easy. You are trusting people to take action on their own.

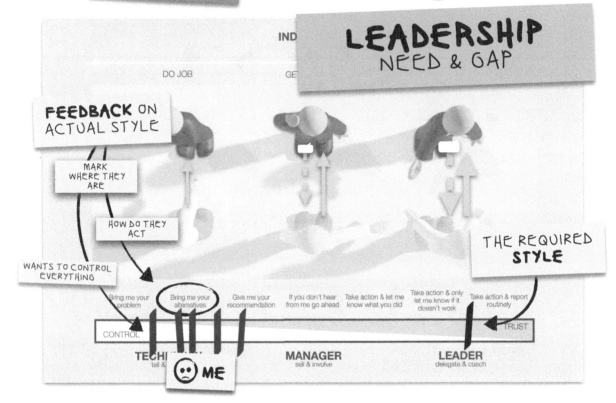

...OPLE Map

PROBLEM
CAPTURING CURRENT
LEADERSHIP STYLE & ISSUES.

LEADERSHIP
NEED & GAP

FEEDBACK ON
ACTUAL STYLE

MARK
WHERE THEY
ARE

HOW DO THEY
ACT

WANTS TO CONTROL
EVERYTHING

THE REQUIRED
STYLE

INDIVIDUAL

DO JOB

GET

| Bring me your problem | Bring me your alternatives | Give me your recommendation | If you don't hear from me go ahead | Take action & let me know what you did | Take action & only let me know if it doesn't work | Take action & report routinely |

CONTROL

TRUST

TECHNICIAN
tell & ...

MANAGER
sell & involve

LEADER
delegate & coach

☹ ME

use for...
Identifying the current & required
leadership style.

tips
Individuals may not want to risk
giving you honest feedback.

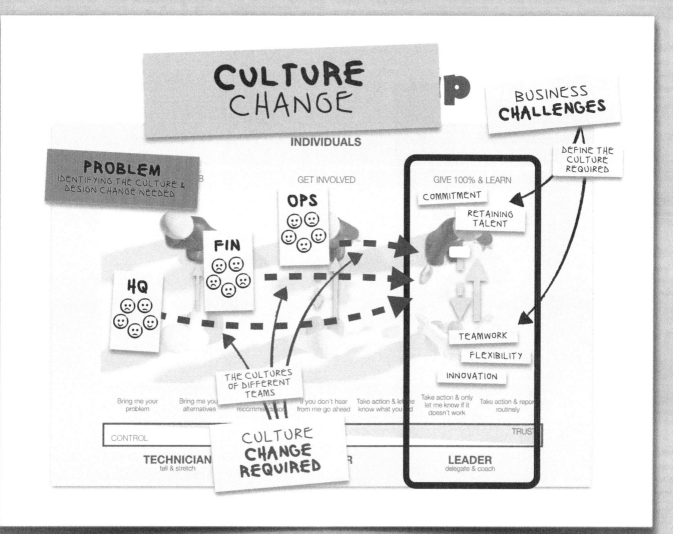

use for...

Defining the required culture & the change required.

tips

The way individual teams work will often reflect the style of their leader.

EMPLOYEE ENGAGEMENT

TEAM DEVELOPMENT

LEADERSHIP & CULTURE

CULTURE CHANGE

Remember people aren't always going to tell you that they are not engaged, not doing their best or that you are a rubbish leader.

They will tell you if they trust you. You may have to disclose your thoughts/feelings first.

So you need to listen hard, observe body language and value anyone that has the courage to be honest about how things are.

real
examples

Now lets have a look at some examples of the tool (principles) in action to solve a range of people problems :

- ☐ **company turnaround** - where listening to the concerns of disengaged employees was critical.

- ☐ **equipping leaders** - equipping his leadership team for future change.

- ☐ **large enterprise** - how a culture & leadership style was identified.

- ☐ **culture change** - defining a new culture & what it would look like at different tiers (layers).

COMPANY TURNAROUND & **EMPLOYEE ENGAGEMENT**

PROBLEM
Understanding why employees
were not engaged

PEOPLE Map

DELIVERY REALITIES
Why there might not be
enough trust (or energy) to
implement any changes

HONEST COMMUNICATION
People needed to know why they
should change or get involved

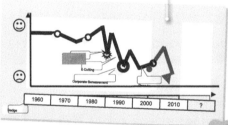

The Companies Story

What's happening NOW

LISTENING & UNDERSTANDING
How employees feel & past experience
that had led to little trust in management
& a fear for their future

VISUALISE & ACKNOWLEDGE
Showing directors where their people are
& understand why they feel that way

SOLUTION
Employees were understood, their
issues/ideas listened to, actioned &
trust was gradually re-build.

Re-engaging & Involving Employees (2011)

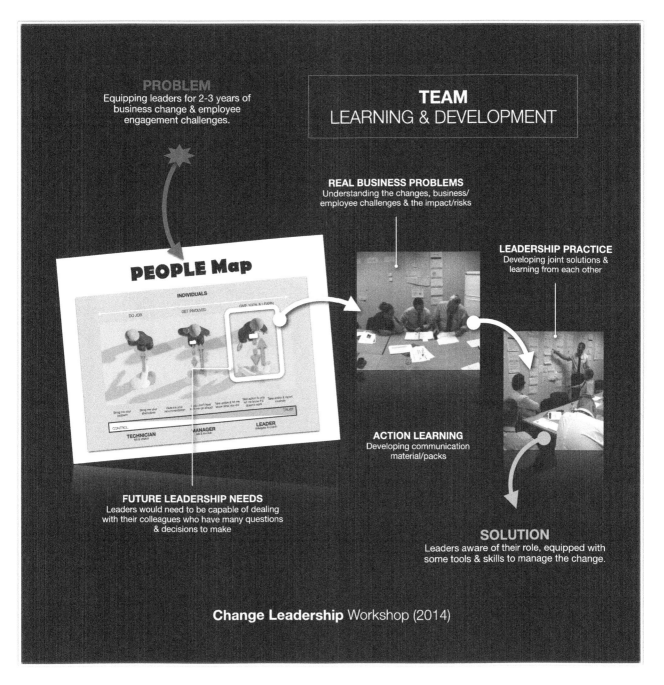

PROBLEM
Equipping leaders for 2-3 years of business change & employee engagement challenges.

TEAM
LEARNING & DEVELOPMENT

REAL BUSINESS PROBLEMS
Understanding the changes, business/employee challenges & the impact/risks

LEADERSHIP PRACTICE
Developing joint solutions & learning from each other

PEOPLE Map

INDIVIDUALS

ACTION LEARNING
Developing communication material/packs

FUTURE LEADERSHIP NEEDS
Leaders would need to be capable of dealing with their colleagues who have many questions & decisions to make

SOLUTION
Leaders aware of their role, equipped with some tools & skills to manage the change.

Change Leadership Workshop (2014)

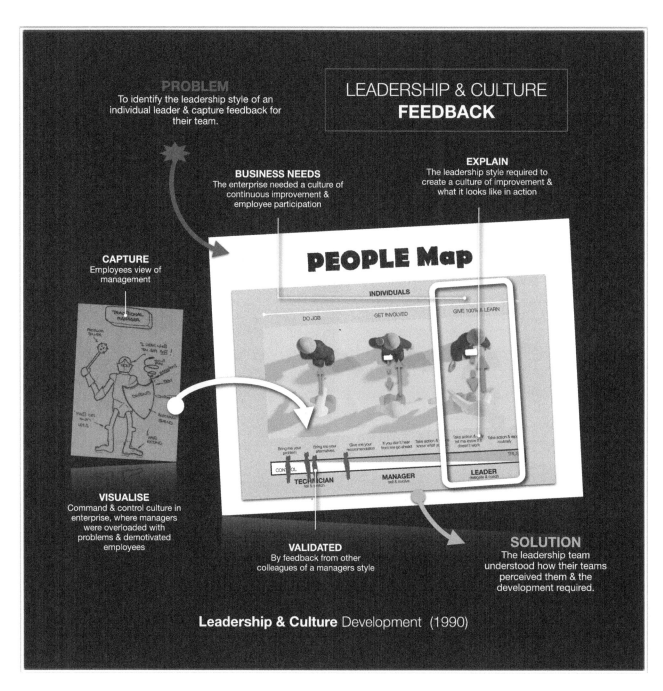

PROBLEM
To identify the leadership style of an individual leader & capture feedback for their team.

LEADERSHIP & CULTURE
FEEDBACK

BUSINESS NEEDS
The enterprise needed a culture of continuous improvement & employee participation

EXPLAIN
The leadership style required to create a culture of improvement & what it looks like in action

CAPTURE
Employees view of management

PEOPLE Map

INDIVIDUALS

DO JOB   GET INVOLVED   GIVE 100% & LEARN

Bring me your problem   Bring me your alternatives   Give me your recommendation   If you don't hear from me go ahead   Take action & know what you   Take action & let me know if it doesn't work   Take action & report routinely

CONTROL

TECHNICIAN
tell & match

MANAGER
tell & involve

LEADER
delegate & coach

VISUALISE
Command & control culture in enterprise, where managers were overloaded with problems & demotivated employees

VALIDATED
By feedback from other colleagues of a managers style

SOLUTION
The leadership team understood how their teams perceived them & the development required.

Leadership & Culture Development (1990)

PROBLEM
Defining the new culture, the level of
empowerment & what is expected in the
organisation.

CULTURE CHANGE &
EMPOWERMENT REALITIES

THE CULTURE IN ACTION
How things will look in action

COMMUNICATE
What team work will look like
in action & making the new
culture tangible

Engineering VISION

Map

Fleet Restructuring	Decision Making	Culture in Action

Self Directed Teams

PRODUCTION

Performance Management

Operational (Minute to Week)
- Manage Roster
- Develop Work Method
- Write + Improve (ISO 9000) Work Instructions
- Control Work Quality (SPC)
- Analyse + Improve Service Performance
- Housekeeping + Safety
- Develop Investment Ideas
- Training Plan (+Budget)
- Recognition + Discipline
- Manage Budget (Tools etc)

Tactical (Week to Year)
- Customer Needs (+ Response)
- Setting Supplier Goals (+ Contract review)
- Set Targets + Priorities
- Set Standards
- Production Scheduling
- Develop & Audit Procedures (ISO9000)
- Re-engineer Work Processes
- Employee Appraisals + Coaching
- Produce Communications
- Produce Investment Reports
- Reward + Discipline

Continuous Improvement

LEADER

UNDERSTANDING
The organisation structure formed of the
work team & the new leadership roles

DEFINING EMPOWERMENT
Identifying what different roles/tiers are
responsible for & decision they can take

SOLUTION
The teams & managers are
empowered to make decisions.

Organisation Structure & the **New Culture** (1997)

review

You can now quickly understand where people in the enterprise are, how engaged they are and how you can empower them. As a leader you can identify your style and it's link to culture. Now you can :

get **the best from people**

Using this tool will help you develop your ability to interview (understand individuals), influence others (motivate them) and build teams (get individuals to collaborate).

people

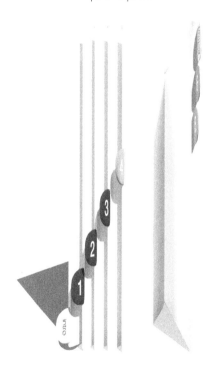

SKILLS

Inspiring (Role Model)
Involving (Empower)
Engaging (Empathy)
Developing Others (Coaching)
Learning (Seeks Feedback & Help)
Self Awareness (Ability & Limits)
Team Building (Collaboration) ✓
Influencing (Motivation) ✓
Interviewing (Individuals) ✓
Improving (Performance)
Organising (Resources)
Planning (Path & Priorities)
Decision Making (Choices)
Problem Solving (Create/Design)
Analysing (Cause/Effect)
Identifying (Opportunities/Problems)
Listening (Collect Info)
Questioning (Research)

↑

practice using the
tool to develop
these skills

TOOL

↑

understanding
people, teams &
organisations

5

leader

leader

developing others

leader

All enterprises need to have good & effective leadership to become & continue to be successful. By understanding how leadership works, the skills involved & the development process, we will be able to see how to develop ourselves & leaders in our enterprise. So let's take a moment & start :

- ☐ understanding **how leadership works**
- ☐ assessing **your performance** & skills
- ☐ creating a personal **development plan**

After understanding how leadership works we will be able to identify our own & our peoples leadership skills, create a development plan & implement good leadership in our enterprise effectively. So let's explore leadership in our enterprise & see how we can make it better.

problem

5

developing
others

assessing
myself & others

how do i
develop myself

performance
management &
succession

fast knowledge

To get the best from others (**leadership**), we need to understand how good we are (**self awareness**), what we need to learn (**skills involved**) and how to keep learning (**development**).

Now let's turn this knowledge into a picture.

leadership

developing others

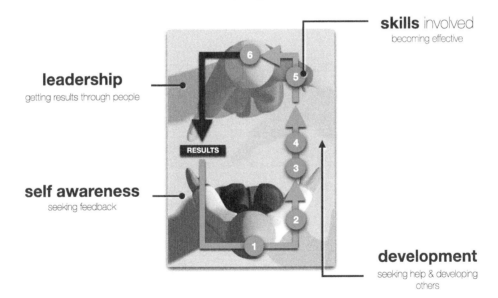

skills involved
becoming effective

leadership
getting results through people

RESULTS

self awareness
seeking feedback

development
seeking help & developing others

leadership
getting result through people

A leader is a person who guides others. They use their ability to **influence** others to deliver/execute the plan & get people to give their best. They **get results** by inspiring people to do things, this will involve being both challenging & supportive.

influence

get results

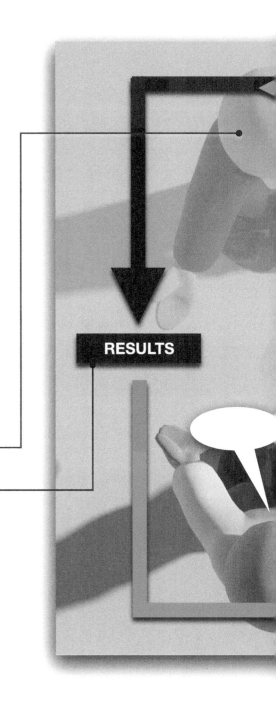

RESULTS

self awareness
seeking feedback

To find out how effective a leader we are, we need to understand the impact we have on others. We need to **ask for feedback.** This self knowledge allows us to understand **how good we really are** & identify areas to work on.

ask for feedback

how good we really are

skills involved
becoming effective

To improve our (or others) performance we need to use the feedback to identify **specific skill** gaps & create a development plan. To continually develop we should regularly review performance & update our development plan.

leadership skills

management skills

problem solving skills

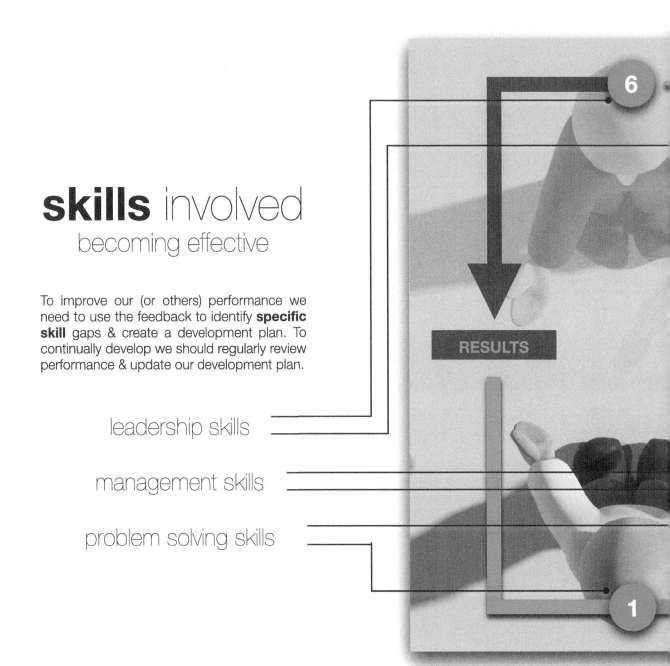

RESULTS

6

1

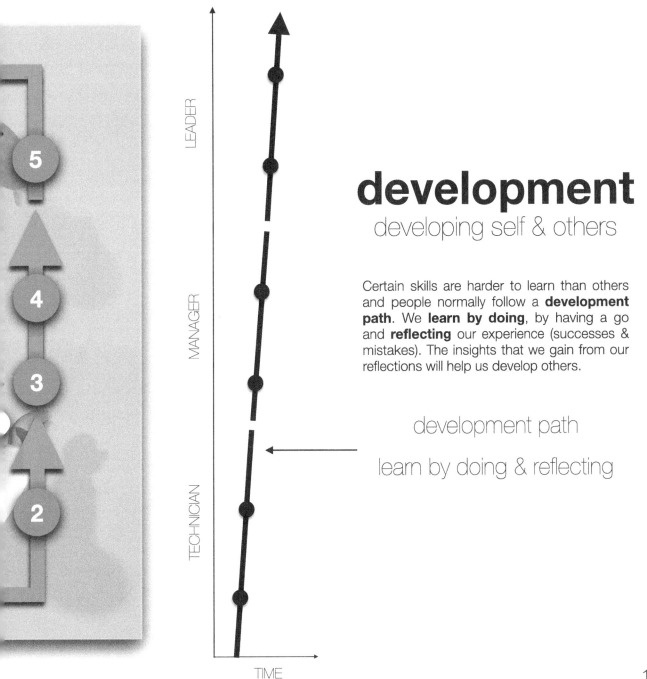

development
developing self & others

Certain skills are harder to learn than others and people normally follow a **development path**. We **learn by doing**, by having a go and **reflecting** our experience (successes & mistakes). The insights that we gain from our reflections will help us develop others.

development path

learn by doing & reflecting

LEADER

MANAGER

TECHNICIAN

TIME

practical tool

Now we can take our knowledge of leadership & create a tool. Then use it to solve four common problems.

The tool can be used for several human resource processes, recruitment, performance management, learning & development etc.

It's really useful for interviewing, for thinking about questions to ask, quickly collecting their answers & your assessment.

LEADER Map

YOU CAN CREATE THIS TOOL BY JUST USING STICK ITS

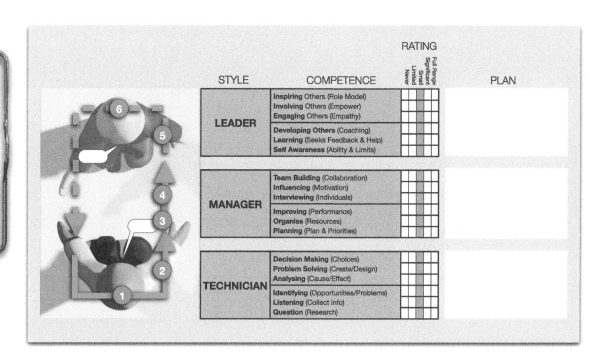

STYLE	COMPETENCE	RATING Never / Limited / Small / Significant / Full Range	PLAN
LEADER	**Inspiring** Others (Role Model) **Involving** Others (Empower) **Engaging** Others (Empathy) **Developing Others** (Coaching) **Learning** (Seeks Feedback & Help) **Self Awareness** (Ability & Limits)		
MANAGER	**Team Building** (Collaboration) **Influencing** (Motivation) **Interviewing** (Individuals) **Improving** (Performance) **Organise** (Resources) **Planning** (Plan & Priorities)		
TECHNICIAN	**Decision Making** (Choices) **Problem Solving** (Create/Design) **Analysing** (Cause/Effect) **Identifying** (Opportunities/Problems) **Listening** (Collect Info) **Question** (Research)		

☐ Work your way up the tool & mark where you think **you are** at.
☐ Draw up a development action for the **key gaps** & identify your support team.
☐ Review your **progress** every few months & plot the movement.

SELF APPRAISAL

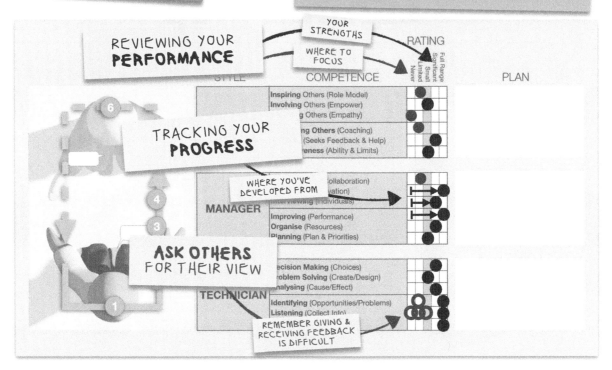

use for...
Assessing yourself or an individuals performance & skills. Can also be used for interviews.

tips
Ask others to score you & think about the variations (perception/reality).

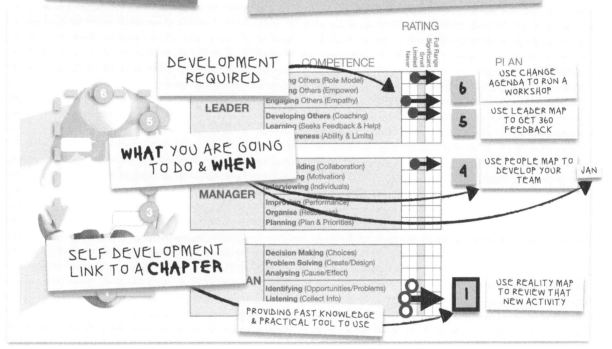

DEVELOPMENT PLAN

RATING

DEVELOPMENT REQUIRED

COMPETENCE

	Never	Limited	Small	Significant	Full Range

PLAN

...ng Others (Role Model)

...ng Others (Empower)

Engaging Others (Empathy)

LEADER

Developing Others (Coaching)

Learning (Seeks Feedback & Help)

...areness (Ability & Limits)

6 USE CHANGE AGENDA TO RUN A WORKSHOP

5 USE LEADER MAP TO GET 360 FEEDBACK

WHAT YOU ARE GOING TO DO & WHEN

...ilding (Collaboration)

...ng (Motivation)

...terviewing (Individuals)

MANAGER

Improving (Performance)

Organise (Res...)

Planning (Plan & Priorities)

4 USE PEOPLE MAP TO DEVELOP YOUR TEAM   JAN

SELF DEVELOPMENT LINK TO A **CHAPTER**

Decision Making (Choices)

Problem Solving (Create/Design)

Analysing (Cause/Effect)

Identifying (Opportunities/Problems)

Listening (Collect Info)

...AN

1 USE REALITY MAP TO REVIEW THAT NEW ACTIVITY

PROVIDING FAST KNOWLEDGE & PRACTICAL TOOL TO USE

use for...

Creating a personal development plan.

tips

Remember we all learn in different ways & at different speeds.

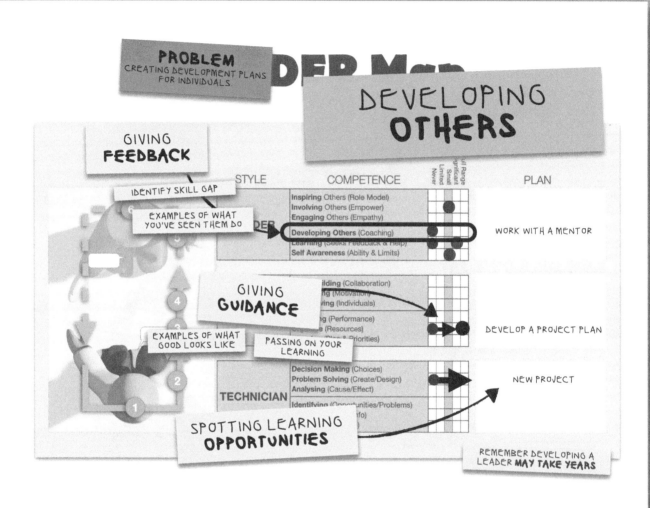

PROBLEM
CREATING DEVELOPMENT PLANS
FOR INDIVIDUALS.

DER Map

DEVELOPING
OTHERS

GIVING
FEEDBACK

IDENTIFY SKILL GAP

EXAMPLES OF WHAT
YOU'VE SEEN THEM DO

GIVING
GUIDANCE

EXAMPLES OF WHAT
GOOD LOOKS LIKE

PASSING ON YOUR
LEARNING

SPOTTING LEARNING
OPPORTUNITIES

STYLE	COMPETENCE	Never	Limited Small	Significant	Full Range	PLAN
	Inspiring Others (Role Model)					
	Involving Others (Empower)			●		
	Engaging Others (Empathy)					
	Developing Others (Coaching)		●	● ●		WORK WITH A MENTOR
	Learning (Seeks Feedback & Help)			●		
	Self Awareness (Ability & Limits)					
	...lding (Collaboration)					
	...g (Motivation)					
	...ving (Individuals)			●		
	...g (Performance)					
	...e (Resources)		● ●	●		DEVELOP A PROJECT PLAN
	...& Priorities)					
	Decision Making (Choices)					
	Problem Solving (Create/Design)					NEW PROJECT
TECHNICIAN	Analysing (Cause/Effect)					
	Identifying (Opportunities/Problems)					

REMEMBER DEVELOPING A
LEADER **MAY TAKE YEARS**

use for...
Reviewing an individuals
performance or carrying out a
formal employee appraisal.

tips
Preparation is important, you need
to identify specific skill gaps &
explain what good looks like.

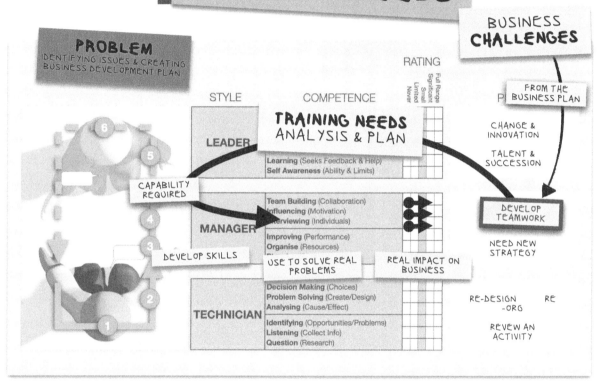

BUSINESS **NEEDS**

BUSINESS CHALLENGES

PROBLEM
IDENTIFYING ISSUES & CREATING
BUSINESS DEVELOPMENT PLAN

RATING

FROM THE
BUSINESS PLAN

STYLE	COMPETENCE		Never	Limited	Small	Significant	Full Range

TRAINING NEEDS
ANALYSIS & PLAN

CHANGE &
INNOVATION

TALENT &
SUCCESSION

LEADER

Learning (Seeks Feedback & Help)
Self Awareness (Ability & Limits)

CAPABILITY
REQUIRED

Team Building (Collaboration)
Influencing (Motivation)
Interviewing (Individuals)

DEVELOP
TEAMWORK

NEED NEW
STRATEGY

MANAGER

Improving (Performance)
Organise (Resources)

DEVELOP SKILLS

USE TO SOLVE REAL
PROBLEMS

REAL IMPACT ON
BUSINESS

RE-DESIGN   RE
-ORG

Decision Making (Choices)
Problem Solving (Create/Design)
Analysing (Cause/Effect)

REVIEW AN
ACTIVITY

TECHNICIAN

Identifying (Opportunities/Problems)
Listening (Collect Info)
Question (Research)

use for...
Identifying future training &
development needs.

tips
Look for leaders in the enterprise
who can be role models & mentors.

TEAM APPRAISAL

SUCCESSION

HIGHER EDUCATION

BUSINESS NEEDS

Note that we will only be given feedback if others think we are willing to accept it & do something with it.

This tool can help you pass on your personal hard won wisdom (mistakes) and develop others and release their potential.

real
examples

Now lets have a look at some examples of the tool in action to solve a range of leadership problems. :

- ☐ **leadership team** - how the development needs of a leadership team was identified.

- ☐ **succession** - how a small business managed a change of leadership.

- ☐ **education** - design an entrepreneurship education module for graduates.

- ☐ **large enterprises** - business needs into required leadership capabilities & development.

PROBLEM
Identifying the leadership development
needs for a team & develop learning
solutions.

APPRAISALS
Fast performance reviews for all
team members to establish their
development needs

LEADERS
Names of individual
team members

GROUP DEVELOPMENT
All leaders need to develop these
skills so group session will be used

LEADER Map

SOLUTION
Training needs identified & a
Leadership Programme developed
to fill the gaps.

IDENTIFYING STRENGTHS & GAPS
Black indicates a strength, grey is ok & white
is a development need

PEER TRAINING
Individuals who have these skills
can develop & mentor others

Team Development in action (2014)

PROBLEM
Existing director has to leave the business &
a new director (successor) to be developed
quickly.

DEVELOPMENT PLAN
Real business problems as learning
opportunities, action plan & support identified

ACTION LEARNING
Created a vision wall to communicate &
develop the plan. Involving the team
created further personal learning

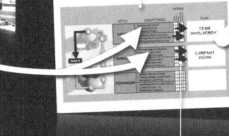

LEADER Map

IDENTIFY NEEDS
Business issues & ideas including new
directors personal reflections on
themselves & the team

ASSESS ABILITY
Directors development needs

SOLUTION
Implemented development plan
with ongoing mentoring support.

Fast Director Development in action (2010)

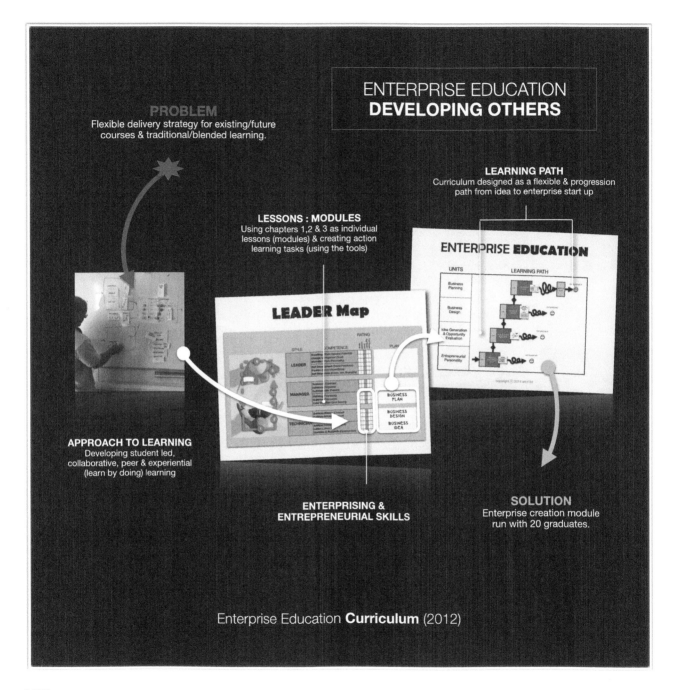

ENTERPRISE EDUCATION
DEVELOPING OTHERS

PROBLEM
Flexible delivery strategy for existing/future
courses & traditional/blended learning.

LEARNING PATH
Curriculum designed as a flexible & progression
path from idea to enterprise start up

LESSONS : MODULES
Using chapters 1,2 & 3 as individual
lessons (modules) & creating action
learning tasks (using the tools)

LEADER Map

APPROACH TO LEARNING
Developing student led,
collaborative, peer & experiential
(learn by doing) learning

**ENTERPRISING &
ENTREPRENEURIAL SKILLS**

SOLUTION
Enterprise creation module
run with 20 graduates.

Enterprise Education **Curriculum** (2012)

PROBLEM
Understanding the leadership required for the future of a business.

BUSINESS TRAINING
NEEDS

LEADER Map

CAPTURE

Major changes in business activities & workload

Leaders required to manage transition period

Maintain employees engaging & manage industrial relations

POSSIBLE FUTURE
Working with the leader to identify future scenarios & business changes

REQUIRED SKILLS & TOOLS
To help managers manage in the future

SOLUTION
Required (future) leadership capabilities identified.

Organisation Development in action (2014)

review

Now you understand how leadership works and the skills involved, you can start to plan your development. Developing yourself will help you identify talent and develop others. You can now :

develop yourself & leaders

Using this tool will help you develop self awareness (understand your ability & limits), learn more effectively (by seeking feedback & help) and develop others (passing on your learning by coaching).

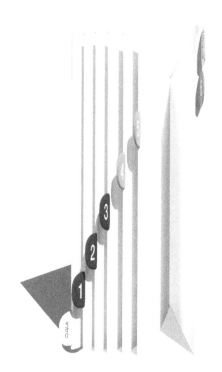

SKILLS

Inspiring (Role Model)
Involving (Empower)
Engaging (Empathy)

Developing Others (Coaching) ✓
Learning (Seeks Feedback & Help) ✓
Self Awareness (Ability & Limits) ✓

Team Building (Collaboration)
Influencing (Motivation)
Interviewing (Individuals)

Improving (Performance)
Organising (Resources)
Planning (Path & Priorities)

Decision Making (Choices)
Problem Solving (Create/Design)
Analysing (Cause/Effect)

Identifying (Opportunities/Problems)
Listening (Collect Info)
Questioning (Research)

TOOL

practice using the
tool to develop
these skills

develop yourself &
others

6

change

change

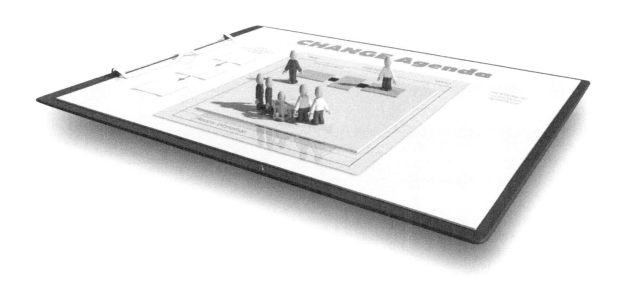

doing things differently

change

All enterprises have to keep changing to become & continue to be successful. By understanding how change works, we will be able to see how to implement changes to our enterprise. So let's take a moment & look how change works by :

- ☐ understanding **the process of change**
- ☐ creating **commitment & ownership**
- ☐ **continually improving**

After understanding how change works we will be able to adjust, adapt & manage our enterprise through the constant changes, involving all our people. So let's explore how change will work in our enterprise & see how we can do things differently.

problem

6

doing things
differently

making change stick	little or no innovation	involving employees

fast knowledge

To do things differently (**a new way**) we need to be dis-satisfied with the present (**where are we now**), have a vision of a better way (**where are we going**) and have some ideas about making it happen (**getting there**).

Now let's turn this knowledge into a picture

change

doing things differently

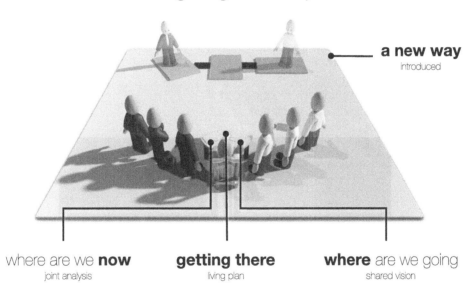

a new way
introduced

where are we **now**
joint analysis

getting there
living plan

where are we going
shared vision

where are we **now**
joint analysis

Change starts with a dis-satisfaction with the way things are & an understanding of all the current **issues & concerns**. This review process (analysis) explains why change is important and will trigger **what if & why not** questions and an active search for opportunities.

issues & concerns

what if & why not

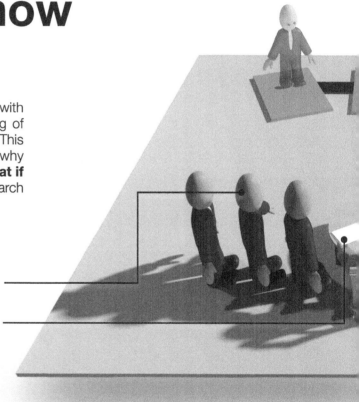

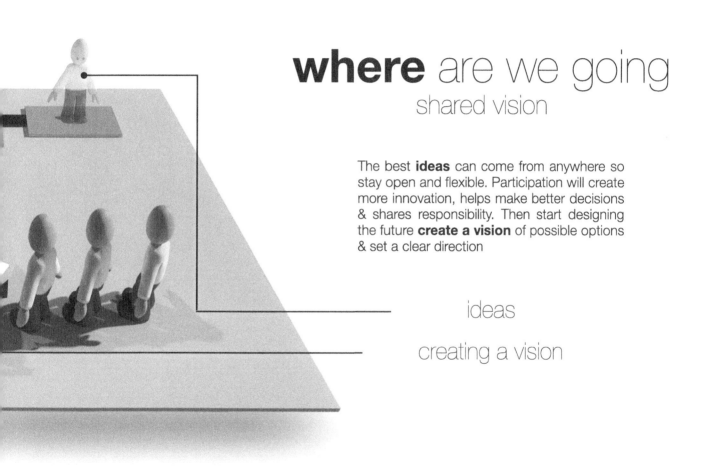

where are we going
shared vision

The best **ideas** can come from anywhere so stay open and flexible. Participation will create more innovation, helps make better decisions & shares responsibility. Then start designing the future **create a vision** of possible options & set a clear direction

ideas

creating a vision

getting there
living plan

Real change is messy, it's a process that will involve lots of small steps & learning. We will have to **experiment**, by creating prototypes, running pilots & demonstrating the vision in action. There will be many different **paths** but eventually you'll develop a plan.

experiment ⎯⎯⎯⎯⎯⎯⎯

paths ⎯⎯⎯⎯⎯⎯⎯

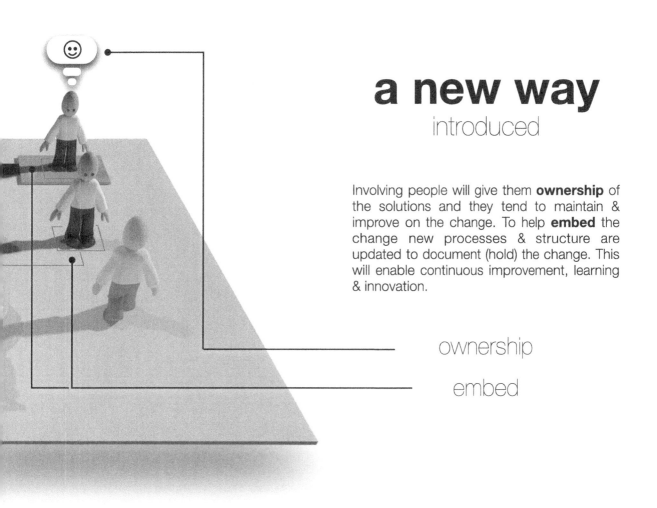

a new way
introduced

Involving people will give them **ownership** of the solutions and they tend to maintain & improve on the change. To help **embed** the change new processes & structure are updated to document (hold) the change. This will enable continuous improvement, learning & innovation.

ownership

embed

practical
tool

Now we can see that change is a journey, that involves understanding where we are, creating a vision and developing a plan to get there.

The tool in this chapter helps you communicate this journey and involve others in creating the (their) future.

YOU CAN CREATE THIS TOOL BY JUST USING STICK ITS

CHANGE Agenda

TOOL
communication
material

TIME	AGENDA	WHO
	Introduction	
	where are we NOW...	
	where are we GOING...	
	how are we going to GET THERE...	
	Review Workshop	

AUDIENCE
concerns
questions

☐ Now think of **the questions** your people are going to raise.
☐ Create your **communication material**, using tools from chapters 1,2 & 3.
☐ Practice giving the presentation, to establish the best **flow & timings**.

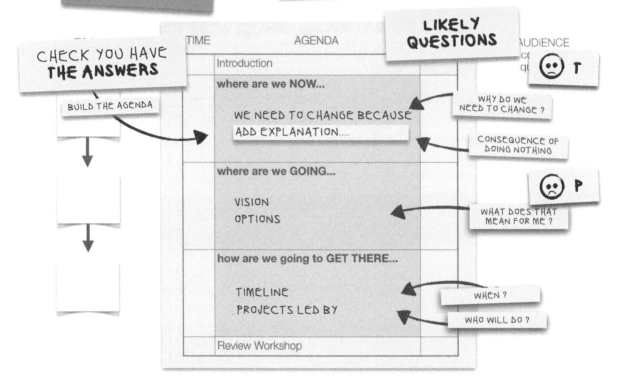

PROBLEM
CAPTURING WHERE PEOPLE ARE, THERE ISSUES & NEEDS.

AUDIENCE

CHANGE

TIME	AGENDA	AUDIENCE

LIKELY QUESTIONS

CHECK YOU HAVE THE ANSWERS

BUILD THE AGENDA

Introduction

where are we NOW...

WE NEED TO CHANGE BECAUSE ADD EXPLANATION....

WHY DO WE NEED TO CHANGE ?

CONSEQUENCE OF DOING NOTHING

where are we GOING...

VISION
OPTIONS

WHAT DOES THAT MEAN FOR ME ?

how are we going to GET THERE...

TIMELINE
PROJECTS LED BY

WHEN ?

WHO WILL DO ?

Review Workshop

T

P

use for...
Identifying the audience needs & expectations and how you would answer them.

tips
People will want to know what the change means for their job & their future.

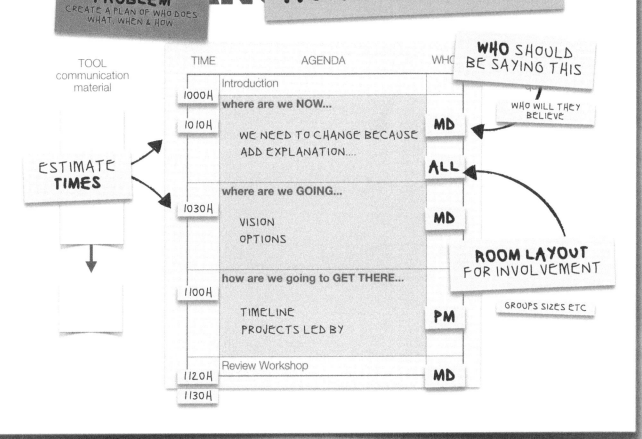

RUNNING ORDER

PROBLEM
CREATE A PLAN OF WHO DOES WHAT, WHEN & HOW

TOOL
communication material

ESTIMATE TIMES

TIME	AGENDA	WHO
	Introduction	
1000H	**where are we NOW...**	
1010H		MD
	WE NEED TO CHANGE BECAUSE ADD EXPLANATION....	
		ALL
	where are we GOING...	
1030H		MD
	VISION	
	OPTIONS	
	how are we going to GET THERE...	
1100H		
	TIMELINE	PM
	PROJECTS LED BY	
	Review Workshop	
1120H		MD
1130H		

WHO SHOULD BE SAYING THIS

WHO WILL THEY BELIEVE

ROOM LAYOUT FOR INVOLVEMENT

GROUPS SIZES ETC

use for...
Creating an agenda & deciding who should be involved in the discussion.

tips
Room layouts have a big impact on dynamic of the group & the level of involvement.

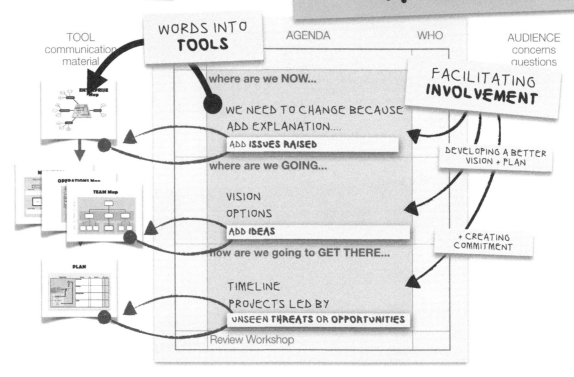

use for...

Developing communication material & capture peoples thoughts.

tips

Use handouts to let people take notes & add their own thinking. It also helps them communicate to people not involved.

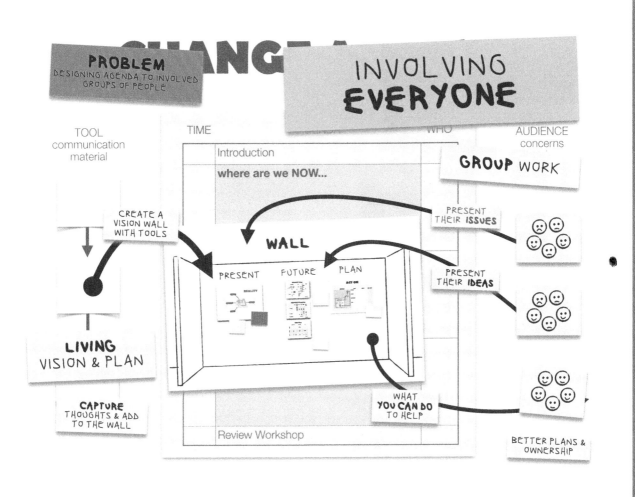

PROBLEM
DESIGNING AGENDA TO INVOLVED
GROUPS OF PEOPLE

INVOLVING EVERYONE

TOOL
communication
material

TIME

WHO

AUDIENCE
concerns

Introduction

where are we NOW...

GROUP WORK

CREATE A
VISION WALL
WITH TOOLS

WALL

PRESENT
THEIR **ISSUES**

PRESENT   FUTURE   PLAN

REALITY

ACT ON

PRESENT
THEIR **IDEAS**

LIVING
VISION & PLAN

CAPTURE
THOUGHTS & ADD
TO THE WALL

WHAT
YOU CAN DO
TO HELP

Review Workshop

BETTER PLANS &
OWNERSHIP

use for...

Creating an interactive display (wall)
to quickly communicate & capture
new issues/ideas.

tips

Create communication walls & turn
offices into living strategies. Walk
people through the plan anytime &
with anyone.

SUCCESSION HANDOVER

LESSON PLAN

SHARING LEARNING

WORKFORCE RESTRUCTURING

Enterprises will always need the ability to create better or more effective product, services, processes, people etc.

The type and size of the change may vary. Either doing the same thing better (improvement) or doing something differently (innovation). Both will involve lots of iteration & learning.

real examples

See the principles and tools being used in a variety of settings, photos to show change in action :

☐ **succession** - how a leadership change was communicated in a small business.

☐ **young entrepreneurs** - a lesson plan designed to engage & equip students.

☐ **social enterprises** - a network of enterprises learning together & supporting each other.

☐ **workforce restructuring** - 1000 employees & unions involved in designing their future jobs.

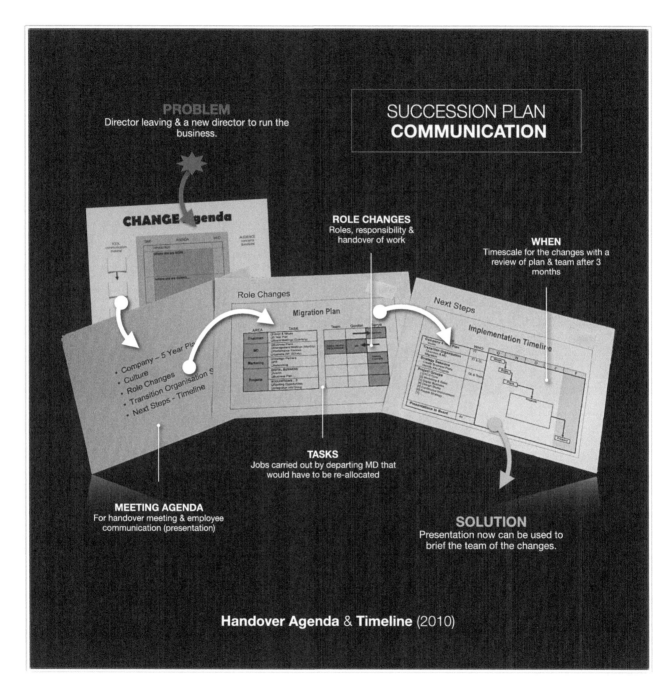

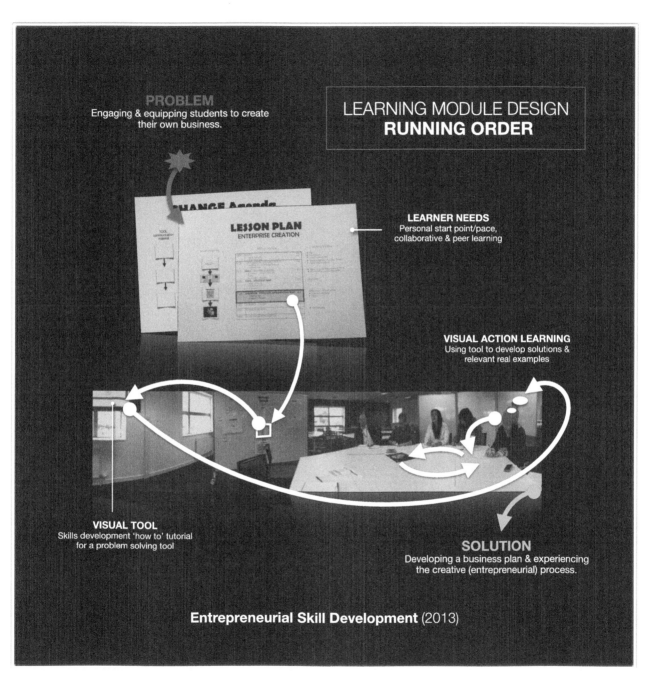

PROBLEM
Engaging & equipping students to create their own business.

LEARNING MODULE DESIGN
RUNNING ORDER

LESSON PLAN
ENTERPRISE CREATION

LEARNER NEEDS
Personal start point/pace, collaborative & peer learning

VISUAL ACTION LEARNING
Using tool to develop solutions & relevant real examples

VISUAL TOOL
Skills development 'how to' tutorial for a problem solving tool

SOLUTION
Developing a business plan & experiencing the creative (entrepreneurial) process.

Entrepreneurial Skill Development (2013)

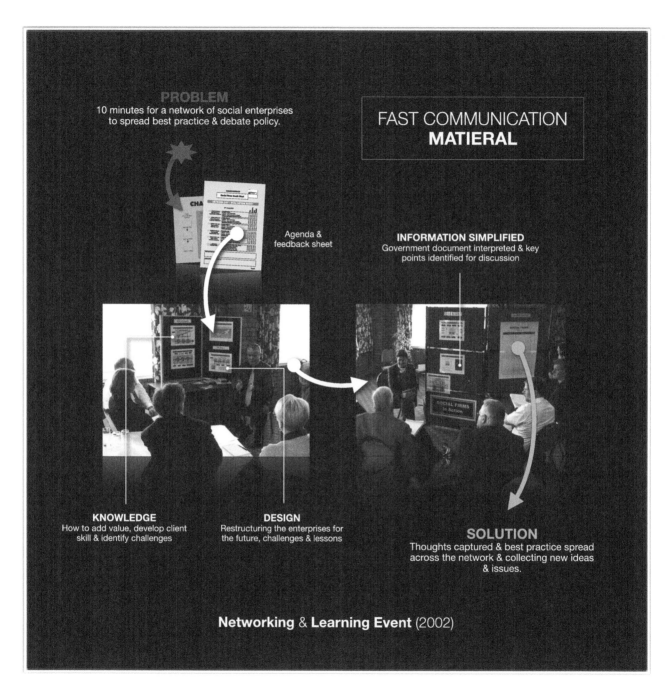

PROBLEM
10 minutes for a network of social enterprises
to spread best practice & debate policy.

FAST COMMUNICATION
MATIERAL

Agenda &
feedback sheet

INFORMATION SIMPLIFIED
Government document interpreted & key
points identified for discussion

KNOWLEDGE
How to add value, develop client
skill & identify challenges

DESIGN
Restructuring the enterprises for
the future, challenges & lessons

SOLUTION
Thoughts captured & best practice spread
across the network & collecting new ideas
& issues.

Networking & **Learning Event** (2002)

INVOLVING **EVERYONE** IN CHANGE

PROBLEM
Helping 1000 employees understanding the new commercial business model & the need for a restructuring deal.

TOOLS & WALLS
Review maps used to explain the big picture & capture employee issues & ideas

WHERE ARE WE NOW
Industry history & privatisation

WHERE ARE WE GOING
The new market place & why the need to change

HOW ARE WE GOING TO GET THERE
Vision, strategy & why restructuring

EMPLOYEE INVOLVEMENT
Jointly designing the future, capturing issues & ideas

The new way of working, new jobs & restructuring & discussion facilitated by the union reps

Fleet Event
November 1996
900 Employees
Six Events

SOLUTION
New business ideas & an improved strategy with a design for a restructuring package & buy in from all employees.

Major Change, **Privatising** & **Restructuring** (1996)

review

We have a picture to explain change, we can now quickly see how to implement, manage & involve our people in the development of the future enterprise. Now you can :

start **implementing solutions**

Using this tool will help you develop your ability to engage an audience (have empathy), involve others (empower them to do things) and inspire action (by role modelling the new way of working).

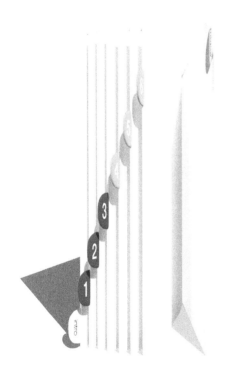

SKILLS

Inspiring (Role Model)	✓
Involving (Empower)	✓
Engaging (Empathy)	✓
Developing Others (Coaching)	
Learning (Seeks Feedback & Help)	
Self Awareness (Ability & Limits)	
Team Building (Collaboration)	
Influencing (Motivation)	
Interviewing (Individuals)	
Improving (Performance)	
Organising (Resources)	
Planning (Path & Priorities)	
Decision Making (Choices)	
Problem Solving (Create/Design)	
Analysing (Cause/Effect)	
Identifying (Opportunities/Problems)	
Listening (Collect Info)	
Questioning (Research)	

TOOL

practice using the
tool to develop
these skills

manage change

case studies

case studies

real life applications

real life applications

All enterprises go through a journey of development, innovation & learning as they grow. By understanding the journeys of other enterprises we will be able to see how we can solve problems, implement change & grow to be successful. So let's look at examples of turning ideas into reality :

- ❑ seeing the tools applied to **complex problems**
- ❑ **learning from** small & big enterprises
- ❑ thinking about **what is possible**

After understanding real enterprise journeys, we will be able to see what problems they encountered, solutions they implemented & how the enterprise changed as a result. You can see what change looks like. So let's explore some real enterprise journeys & see what we can learn from them.

real life

seeing how projects are
tackled & what's possible

toolkit

the tools being used &
examples of actual solutions

some guidance
& tips

the journey from the
vision to reality

link to real
example pages

solving problems &
grabbing opportunities

entrepreneurs start-up

two young founders
turning their **passion** &
talents into an enterprise

tips

Start-ups are built around the founders talents & driven by their idea/vision. As they grow their processes & structure gets stretched & have to be constantly re-designed.

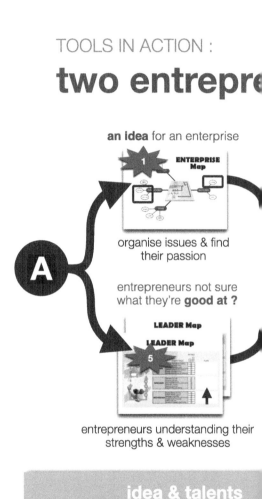

TOOLS IN ACTION :

two entrepre

an idea for an enterprise

ENTERPRISE Map

A

organise issues & find their passion

entrepreneurs not sure what they're **good at ?**

LEADER Map
LEADER Map

entrepreneurs understanding their strengths & weaknesses

idea & talents

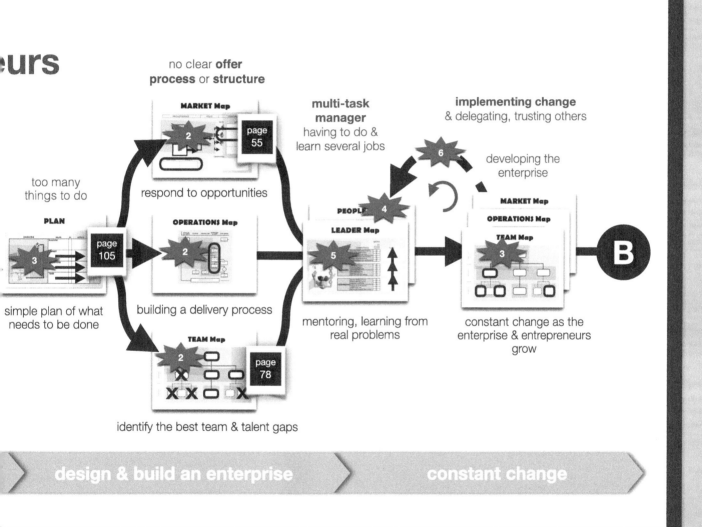

...eurs

no clear **offer process** or **structure**

MARKET Map — page 55

too many things to do

respond to opportunities

PLAN — page 105

simple plan of what needs to be done

OPERATIONS Map

building a delivery process

TEAM Map — page 78

identify the best team & talent gaps

multi-task manager having to do & learn several jobs

PEOPLE

LEADER Map

mentoring, learning from real problems

implementing change & delegating, trusting others

developing the enterprise

MARKET Map

OPERATIONS Map

TEAM Map

B

constant change as the enterprise & entrepreneurs grow

design & build an enterprise   **constant change**

TIMESCALE : 5 years

social enterprises

a group of social
start ups struggling to
develop & **grow**

tips

Social enterprises have a social purpose
meaning that they are caring & commercial.
In this organisation structure & processes
are designed around the abilities &
development of the employees.

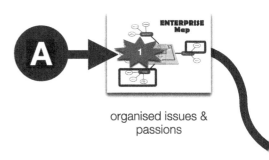

TOOLS IN ACTION :
social enterpr

a group of enterprises
with **a social purpose**

A

organised issues &
passions

social enterpris

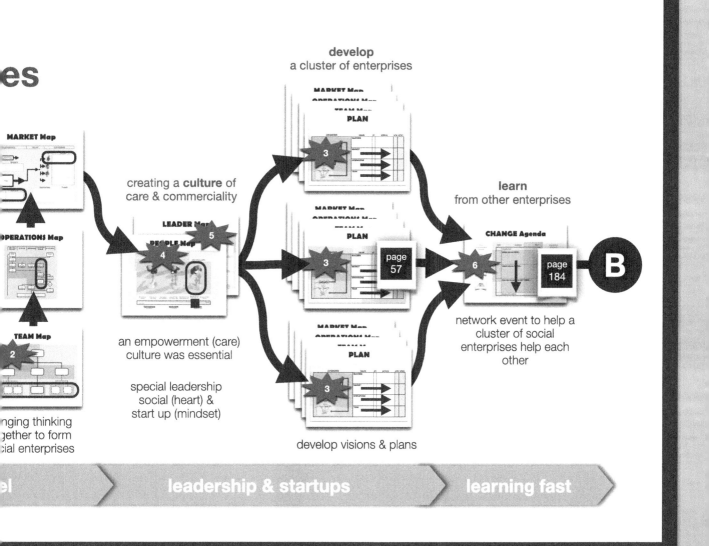

es

develop
a cluster of enterprises

creating a **culture** of
care & commerciality

learn
from other enterprises

an empowerment (care)
culture was essential

special leadership
social (heart) &
start up (mindset)

network event to help a
cluster of social
enterprises help each
other

nging thinking
gether to form
cial enterprises

develop visions & plans

el > **leadership & startups** > **learning fast** >

TIMESCALE : 6 months

succession

replacing the **MD** with another director

tips

Succession is about understanding what the exiting person does & jobs that will be left vacant. A successor needs to know what the plan is, fill the job and develop the missing skills.

TOOLS IN ACTION :

owner succe

fast exit of owner
owner/director has less time for the enterprise

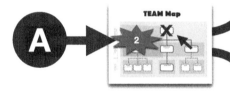

identify role played & gaps left in organisation structure

vacancy gap

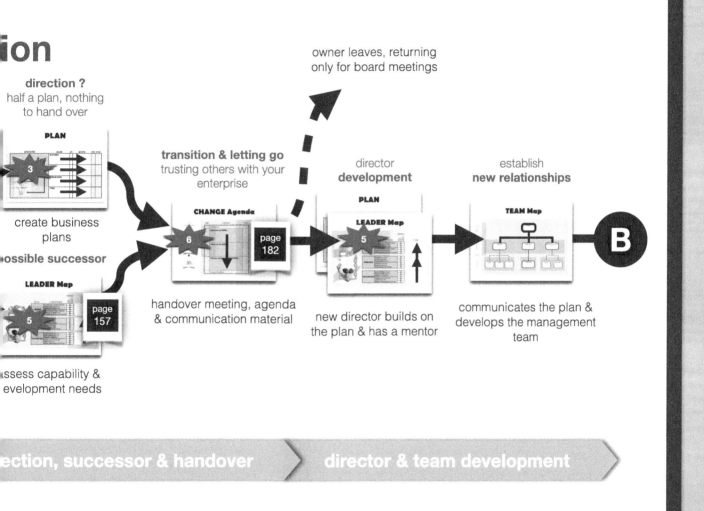

...ion

direction ?
half a plan, nothing
to hand over

PLAN

create business
plans

...ossible successor

LEADER Map

page
157

...ssess capability &
...evelopment needs

owner leaves, returning
only for board meetings

transition & letting go
trusting others with your
enterprise

CHANGE Agenda

page
182

handover meeting, agenda
& communication material

director
development

PLAN

LEADER Map

new director builds on
the plan & has a mentor

establish
new relationships

TEAM Map

B

communicates the plan &
develops the management
team

...ection, successor & handover   **director & team development**

TIMESCALE : 5x 2 hour meetings

199
case studies

employee involvement

how to **involve** the **workforce** in business improvement

tips

Employee involvement is working with the workforce in problem solving & actioning ideas. To keep improving continuously you need to create an empowerment culture & develop the leaders.

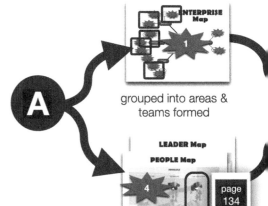

TOOLS IN ACTION :

improvement

employees raise
700 issues

1

grouped into areas &
teams formed

LEADER Map

PEOPLE Map

4

page
134

culture of command & control

identify role models &
train as facilitators

employee inv

A

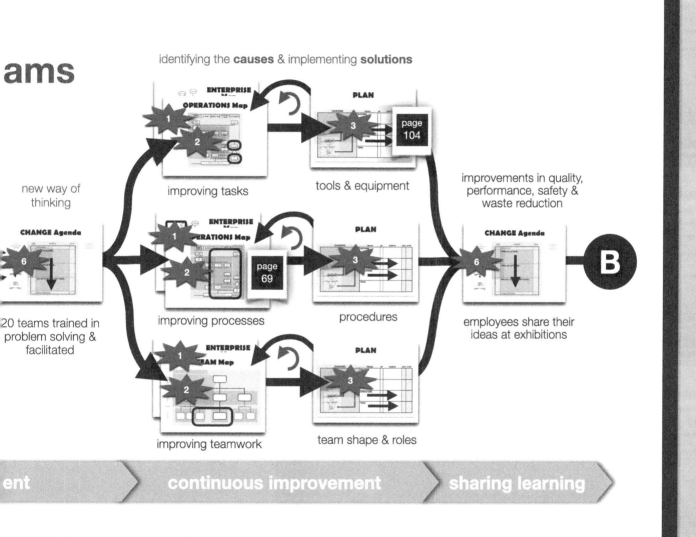

ams

identifying the **causes** & implementing **solutions**

improving tasks

tools & equipment

new way of thinking

20 teams trained in problem solving & facilitated

improving processes

procedures

improvements in quality, performance, safety & waste reduction

employees share their ideas at exhibitions

improving teamwork

team shape & roles

page 104

page 69

CHANGE Agenda

ENTERPRISE OPERATIONS Map

PLAN

ENTERPRISE OPERATIONS Map

PLAN

ENTERPRISE TEAM Map

PLAN

CHANGE Agenda

B

ent

continuous improvement

sharing learning

TIMESCALE : ran for 6 years

restructuring

reducing the workforce
by 20% & **increasing productivity**

tips

Developing a shared vision & involving employees in the design of the organisation speeds up the implementation. Pilots helped develop innovative solutions, show what the vision looks like in action & build commitment.

TOOLS IN ACTION :

restructuring

enterprise to be competitive
increase productivity, reduce costs & release potential of employees

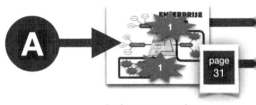

A

page
31

industry promises to the unions
to restructure & improve pay & conditions

shared vision

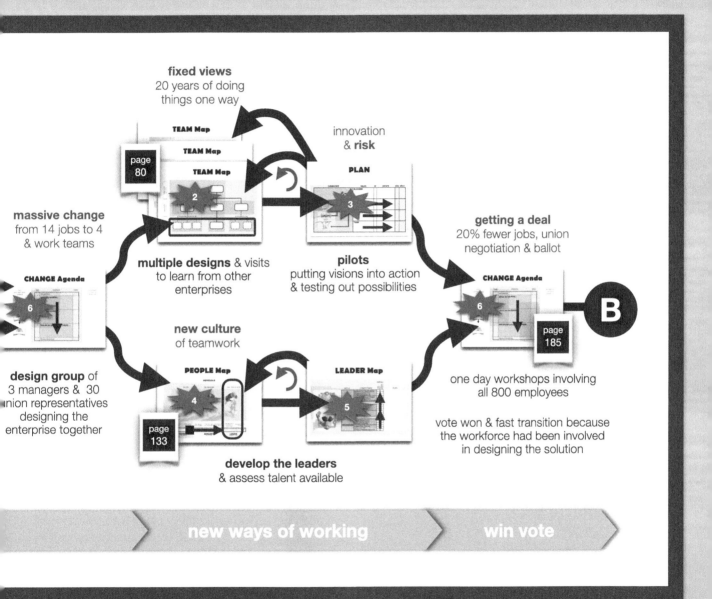

fixed views
20 years of doing things one way

TEAM Map

TEAM Map

page 80

TEAM Map

2

innovation & **risk**

PLAN

3

massive change
from 14 jobs to 4 & work teams

CHANGE Agenda

6

multiple designs & visits to learn from other enterprises

pilots
putting visions into action & testing out possibilities

getting a deal
20% fewer jobs, union negotiation & ballot

CHANGE Agenda

6

page 185

B

new culture
of teamwork

design group of 3 managers & 30 union representatives designing the enterprise together

PEOPLE Map

4

page 133

LEADER Map

5

one day workshops involving all 800 employees

vote won & fast transition because the workforce had been involved in designing the solution

develop the leaders
& assess talent available

new ways of working   win vote

TIMESCALE : design 6 months, negotiation 3 months

203
case studies

privatisation

taking a working public
enterprise & **preparing** it
for the private sector

tips

Designing the organisation from bottom up
and linking all activities with a customer/
supplier chain helped remove waste & align
resources. Involving all managers in
developing options, meant that the
business change was understood, owned
and the culture was changed.

TOOLS IN ACTION :
public to priv

no strategic tier
old public sector
organisation structure

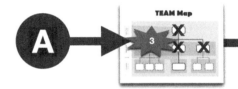

full organisation review
by a team of managers

public sector

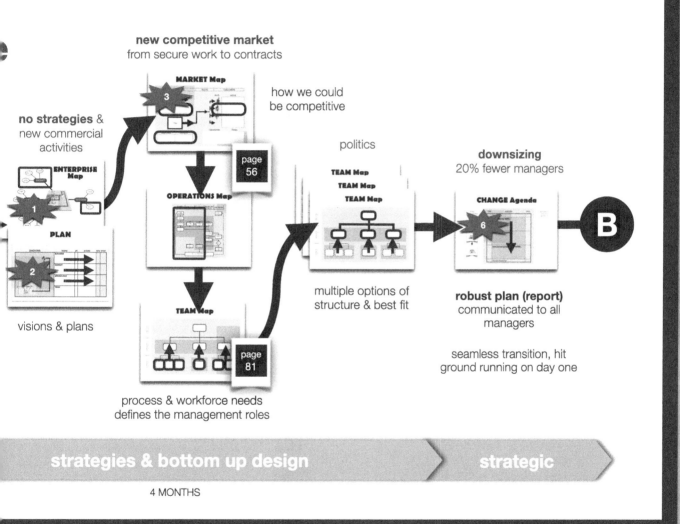

new competitive market
from secure work to contracts

MARKET Map

3

how we could
be competitive

no strategies &
new commercial
activities

ENTERPRISE Map

page 56

politics

downsizing
20% fewer managers

1

OPERATIONS Map

TEAM Map
TEAM Map
TEAM Map

CHANGE Agenda

6

B

PLAN

2

TEAM Map

page 81

multiple options of
structure & best fit

robust plan (report)
communicated to all
managers

visions & plans

process & workforce needs
defines the management roles

seamless transition, hit
ground running on day one

strategies & bottom up design

strategic

4 MONTHS

TIMESCALE : 6 months

company
turnaround

**dis-engaging
employees** & creating a
sustainable enterprise

tips

Engaging (listening to) employees to help
the organisation identify the real problems &
discover hidden talents. Resulting in a living
business plan= developed, written, owned
& implemented by 100+ leaders.

TOOLS IN ACTION :
turnaround

hidden problems
unaware of before takeover

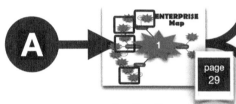

**collecting the real
Issues & ideas**
real time diagnosis of
where the enterprise was

a living plar

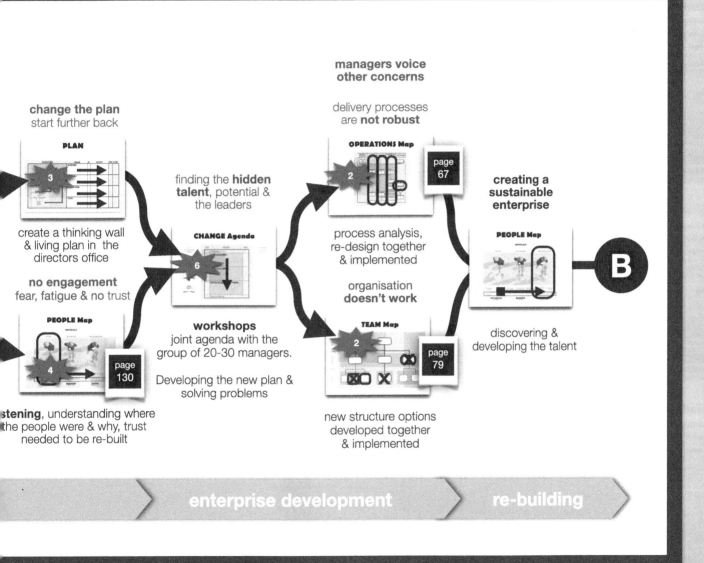

change the plan
start further back

PLAN

3

create a thinking wall
& living plan in the
directors office

no engagement
fear, fatigue & no trust

PEOPLE Map

4

page
130

stening, understanding where
the people were & why, trust
needed to be re-built

finding the **hidden
talent**, potential &
the leaders

CHANGE Agenda

6

workshops
joint agenda with the
group of 20-30 managers.

Developing the new plan &
solving problems

**managers voice
other concerns**

delivery processes
are **not robust**

OPERATIONS Map

2

page
67

process analysis,
re-design together
& implemented

organisation
doesn't work

TEAM Map

2

page
79

new structure options
developed together
& implemented

**creating a
sustainable
enterprise**

PEOPLE Map

B

discovering &
developing the talent

enterprise development   **re-building**

TIMESCALE : 12 months

learning &
development

equipping leaders for
future business
changes

tips

Using real business problems makes
learning relevant, practical and has an
immediate impact on the enterprise & job
holder. Helping leaders to assess
themselves means that development starts
to become self driven & continuous.

TOOLS IN ACTION :
leadership pr

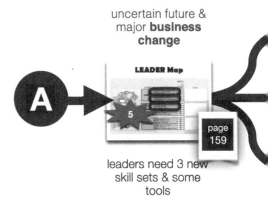

uncertain future &
major **business
change**

leaders need 3 new
skill sets & some
tools

business & individual

ramme

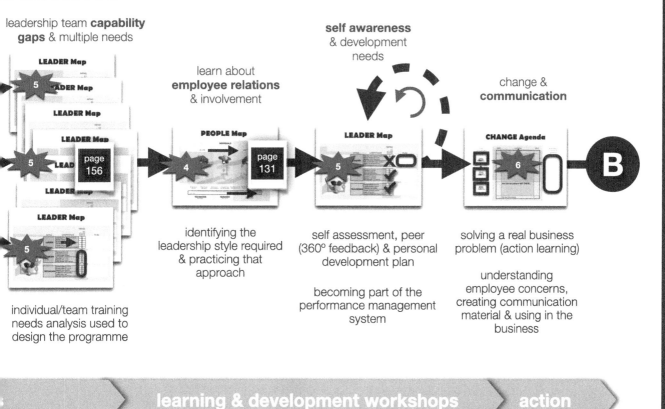

leadership team **capability gaps** & multiple needs

LEADER Map

5

individual/team training needs analysis used to design the programme

learn about **employee relations** & involvement

PEOPLE Map

4 → page 131

identifying the leadership style required & practicing that approach

self awareness & development needs

LEADER Map

5

self assessment, peer (360° feedback) & personal development plan

becoming part of the performance management system

change & **communication**

CHANGE Agenda

6

B

solving a real business problem (action learning)

understanding employee concerns, creating communication material & using in the business

LEADER Map 5 page 156

> **learning & development workshops** > **action**

TIMESCALE : 12 months

209
case studies

entrepreneurship education

developing **enterprising** & **entrepreneurial** graduates

tips

Enterprise education requires students to think in a creative & innovative manner. Visual tools enabled fast business idea development, as well as individualised, collaborative & peer learning.

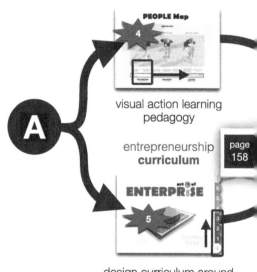

TOOLS IN ACTION :

entrepreneu

traditional education **culture**

PEOPLE Map

4

visual action learning pedagogy

entrepreneurship **curriculum**

page 158

ENTERPRISE

5

design curriculum around the idea to enterprise journey

course desig

A

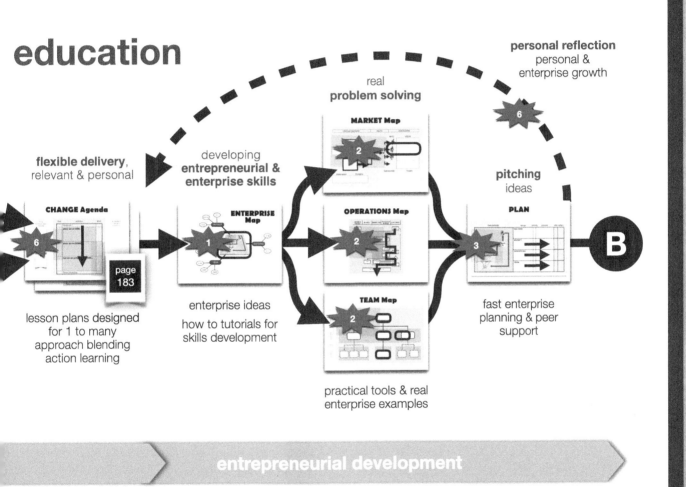

education

personal reflection
personal & enterprise growth

real **problem solving**

flexible delivery, relevant & personal

developing **entrepreneurial & enterprise skills**

pitching ideas

CHANGE Agenda

page 183

ENTERPRISE Map

MARKET Map

OPERATIONS Map

TEAM Map

PLAN

B

lesson plans designed for 1 to many approach blending action learning

enterprise ideas

how to tutorials for skills development

fast enterprise planning & peer support

practical tools & real enterprise examples

entrepreneurial development

TIMESCALE : 12 months

business
support

running **a growing enterprise** or providing business support to them

tips

There are different (but normal) dilemmas at each stage of the enterprise journey (start/ run/grow). Understanding these barriers to growth enables us to address problems early, develop solutions & take action.

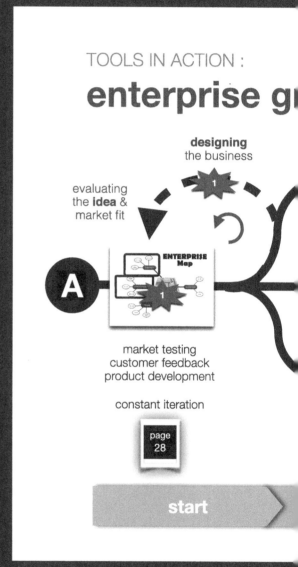

TOOLS IN ACTION :

enterprise gu

designing
the business

evaluating
the **idea** &
market fit

ENTERPRISE
Map

A

market testing
customer feedback
product development

constant iteration

page
28

start

...wth stages

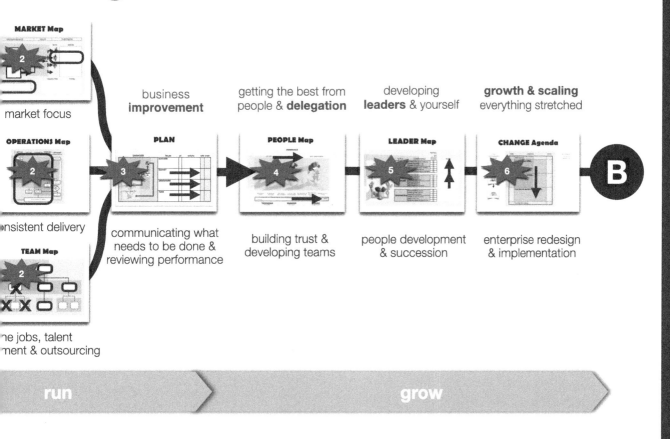

MARKET Map
...market focus

OPERATIONS Map
...nsistent delivery

TEAM Map
...ne jobs, talent
...ment & outsourcing

business
improvement

PLAN

communicating what
needs to be done &
reviewing performance

getting the best from
people & **delegation**

PEOPLE Map

building trust &
developing teams

developing
leaders & yourself

LEADER Map

people development
& succession

growth & scaling
everything stretched

CHANGE Agenda

enterprise redesign
& implementation

B

run

grow

TIMESCALE : the toolkit will help you anticipate & accelerate…

review

You now have an insight and understanding of how real enterprises develop & the innovation journey. You now have everything you need to solve real problems, implement change & build a successful enterprise.

start **unleashing potential**

Using all the tools will develop your ability as a leader & the skills you've learnt will help you turn more ideas into reality. The visual approach will help you engage, equip & empower others…..

SKILLS

Inspiring (Role Model)	
Involving (Empower)	
Engaging (Empathy)	
Developing Others (Coaching)	
Learning (Seeks Feedback & Help)	
Self Awareness (Ability & Limits)	
Team Building (Collaboration)	
Influencing (Motivation)	
Interviewing (Individuals)	
Improving (Performance)	
Organising (Resources)	
Planning (Path & Priorities)	
Decision Making (Choices)	
Problem Solving (Create/Design)	
Analysing (Cause/Effect)	
Identifying (Opportunities/Problems)	
Listening (Collect Info)	
Questioning (Research)	

TOOLKIT

equipped for the
future

start
your journey

The tools in the book are templates to help capture and visualise your (others) thinking. You can create all of the tools in the book with just a pack of stick-its & a piece of paper.

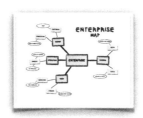

So start creating…

background

background

I spent the first 10 years of my working life as an engineer learning how to invent, make and fix things. I then spent 20 years helping people invent, make and fix enterprises. I did this by just drawing, the picture became :

tools to unleash potential

I started book writing 15 years ago to provide others with the tools to unleash potential. Hopefully I've encouraged you to see & think about things in a new way. To discover things for yourself.

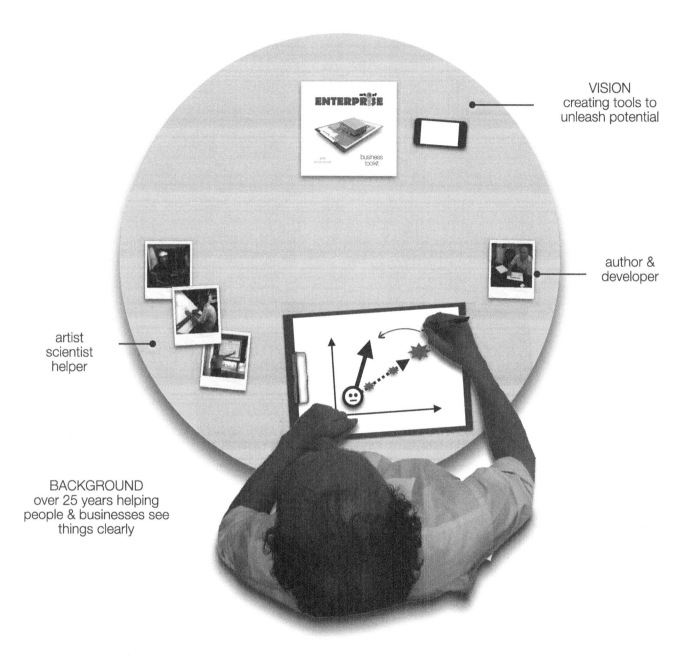

VISION
creating tools to
unleash potential

author &
developer

artist
scientist
helper

BACKGROUND
over 25 years helping
people & businesses see
things clearly

thanks

I started working on the book 15 years ago. We are a family business, the team includes my sons Dan (Editor, Marketing), Joe (Designer, Animator) and Teresa (Director). Without their encouragement, input and hardwork it wouldn't have been possible.

I'd also like to say thanks to those that have given support and advice, including Calvin Germain, Graham Boot-Handford, Andy Cope, Dave Young, Rod Stephens & all the clients I've worked with.

visit us

artofltd.co.uk
@artofenterprise

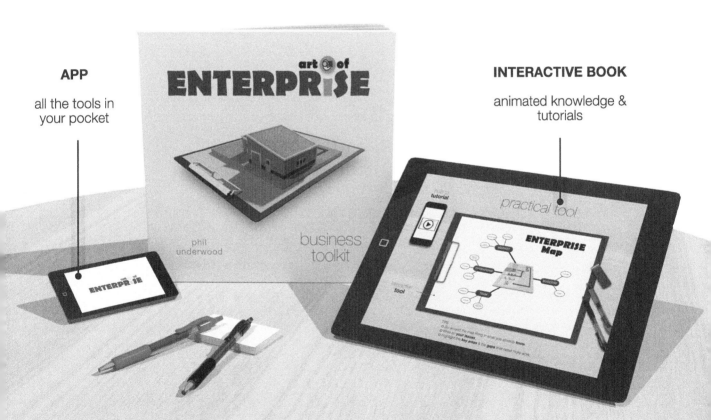

APP

all the tools in
your pocket

INTERACTIVE BOOK

animated knowledge &
tutorials

notes

notes

notes

notes

notes

index

Lightning Source UK Ltd.
Milton Keynes UK
UKOW07f0601250315

248487UK00002B/4/P

9 781910 546000